# Relational Discipline

# Relational Discipline

## Strategies for In-Your-Face Kids

**William N. Bender**

*The University of Georgia*

Boston • New York • San Francisco
Mexico City • Montreal • Toronto • London • Madrid • Munich • Paris
Hong Kong • Singapore • Tokyo • Cape Town • Sydney

**Executive Editor:**  *Virginia Lanigan*
**Editorial Assistant:**  *Erin Liedel*
**Executive Marketing Manager:**  *Amy M. Cronin*
**Manufacturing Buyer:**  *JoAnne Sweeney*
**Production Coordinator:**  *Pat Torelli Publishing Services*
**Editorial-production Service:**  *TKM Productions*
**Electronic Composition:**  *TKM Productions*

For related titles and support materials, visit our online catalog at www.ablongman.com.

**Library of Congress Cataloging-in-Publication Data**

Bender, William N.
    Relational discipline : strategies for in-your-face kids / William N. Bender.
       p.  cm.
    Includes bibliographical references (p.  ) and index.
    ISBN 0-205-30633-0
      1. School discipline--Handbooks, manuals, etc.  2. Teacher-student
relationships--Handbooks, manuals, etc.  I. Title.

LB3012 .B46 2003
371.102'4--dc21                                                     2002019617

Printed in the United States of America

10  9  8  7  6  5  4  3  2  1        06  05  04  03  02

*If you learn nothing else
in your teacher preparation,
do yourself a favor and learn these tactics.
They will save your life in today's classrooms.*

# Contents

# Preface

This book is about "in-your-face" kids—how to manage them, how to teach them, and, most important, how to value them. These are the kids who every teacher dreads and many teachers fear but that certain teachers find affection for, and therein lies our challenge. How can we teachers truly value kids who constantly challenge us?

When I initially considered writing this book on discipline, I was aware of a great deal of concern on the part of teachers about the perception of increasing disciplinary problems in schools. This concern, often voiced in workshops I conduct around the country, is so pervasive and so consistent that I ultimately acknowledged the reality that disciplinary problems in schools have gotten worse in recent years. I have concluded over the last several years that we need an entirely new paradigm for working with in-your-face students, and this book represents my suggestions for such a new perspective. I believe that we need a refocusing—or perhaps an entirely new focus—in discipline, and *Relational Discipline* is the product of investing myself in that endeavor. I have truly enjoyed the intellectual pursuit of formulating a new focus in this area, and as a result of a number of years of experience involved with these issues, I have come to believe certain assumptions.

> Discipline is a relationship that makes a child want to behave in a different fashion.

In simplest terms, discipline is a relationship that makes a child want to behave in a different fashion. Said in a different way, discipline is a relationship that makes a child want to internalize a set of behavioral standards and live in accordance with those standards. This is the very essence of relational discipline. I believe that the critical piece that seems to have been overlooked in most recent books on discipline is the *relationship between the teacher and the student*—a relationship that is fundamental to all our educational efforts, and not merely our disciplinary efforts.

> In positive relationships lie the essence of effective discipline.

Most of us can recall the teacher, coach, mentor, minister, rabbi, or other influential adult in our lives for whom we would jump into a circle of fire. We cared so much about our relationship with that adult that we would attempt the impossible if he or she asked us to. Those adults had a tremendous impact on us and influenced our decisions about how we wanted to behave. The critical aspect in those successful disciplinary situations was the relationship we had with the adult. The relationship made us wish to be someone else, or at least to behave differently in various situations. In such positive relationships lie the essence of effective discipline. I believe that this is one element that we teachers have been missing in our disciplinary efforts.

> If one does not have a positive relationship with a child, one cannot discipline that child.

To extend this relationship concept a bit, I would suggest that if one does not have a positive relationship with a child, one cannot discipline that child. Without the positive relationship, one merely serves a role similar to a police officer—eliciting compliance with certain rules but not disciplining in an effective manner. In this sense, it is useful to distinguish between discipline and the policing functions that teachers must perform. If discipline is dependent on a relationship, then most of what is called "discipline problems" in classrooms and schools are really ineffective policing. Given the present staffing of schools, teachers will always have to perform some essentials "duties" such as bus duty, hall duty, cafeteria duty, and making children follow the rules in those situations. However, I would argue that these are policing functions (i.e., they could be more effectively performed by trained police officers!) and not disciplinary functions, since eliciting compliance on rules is not typically enough to make a child want to internalize those rules. Also, in most nonclassroom duties done by teachers, there is usually no relationship whatsoever between the teacher performing these functions and the student being "disciplined." In short, any teacher may serve in a "policing" role and elicit compliance through various behavioral approaches (rewards, punishments, etc.). And frankly, I have no problem with teachers using these approaches in an ethically responsible fashion for these policing functions.

> If we wish to discipline a child—if we wish for a child to desire to internalize a set of behavioral standards other than what he or she is currently using—we must build a relationship with that child.

Still, I suggest that in order to understand today's problems, we need to differentiate between policing functions and true discipline. If we wish to discipline a child—if we wish for a child to desire to internalize a set of behavioral standards other than what he or she is currently using—we must build a relationship with that child. From this perspective, we teachers must now reevaluate all our current disciplinary plans and ask ourselves: What effect will this or that disciplinary technique have on the relationship between ourselves and the pupil?

I further believe that we haven't considered the significant influence of the peer group in our disciplinary efforts. At some ages (discussed a bit more in Chapter 1), peers are the single most important disciplinary influence in the class—not the teacher. These relationships with a child's peers constitute another emphasis in relational discipline. Although the teacher must assertively set high expectations for appropriate behavior in his or her classroom, the fact is that the peers exercise more disciplinary influence over many in-your-face kids. Thus, we need disciplinary tactics that focus on peer influence as well as teacher influence, and we need careful thought on strategies that are differentially effective at various ages. With this in mind, I have developed a disciplinary approach that focuses developmentally on kids, and I will recommend certain operative strategies for kids of different ages—a developmental perspective on discipline, if you will.

Finally, I must mention that there are personal examples scattered throughout this book. I have studied under a large number of excellent teachers, from my public school education through higher education including Ms. Julia Whitty, Mrs. Thelma Edmonson, Mr. Claude Allen, Mr. Bill Thorington, Mr. Ed Jenkens, and many others. When I mention these teachers, it is with the greatest of respect. To these wonderful teachers and great human beings, I dedicate this book, and I sincerely hope that this effort provides some comfort to the teachers whom I challenged many years ago.

## Acknowledgments

Cartoons, like pictures, can speak volumes. This book is enriched by the illustrations of Ms. Claudia Wood, a talented neighbor, a former teacher, and a friend. A special thanks to her for her insight and her work.

I also thank the following reviewers for their helpful comments: Inge J. Carmola, Director of Special Education, Capital Region BOCES, Albany, New York; Lispbeth E. Gets, School Board of Alchua County; and Amy James, Central Connecticut State University.

## Chapter 1

# Something in the Water?

## The Growing Discipline Problem

Are kids in schools today really behaving differently than they did a few years ago?

Is school violence increasing? Why?

Why do some kids come to school with a gun and, in an unprovoked fashion, begin shooting their teachers and classmates?

Do teachers deal with problems today that were unheard of only a few years ago?

Are kids today less connected to school activities, to each other, and to their families?

Are good teachers leaving the ranks of the public school faculty because of the increase in discipline problems?

Where did attention deficit hyperactivity disorder (ADHD) come from, and why had I not heard about it before 10 years ago?

Can I suspend a kid with behavioral disorders who is violent?

A kid at my school threatened my wife, who taught him a year ago, and the school district won't take action. Is there any way we can protect ourselves?

What is causing the increasing discipline problems? Is there something in the water or what?

These are all real questions that I've been asked repeatedly. Over the last five years or so, I've heard these questions posed by so many parents and teachers, both individually in various social venues as well as in the discipline workshops I conduct, that I became somewhat immune to the real concern, fear, and pain behind these questions. I hate to make such an admission. These repeated concerns voiced by parents and educators, however, caused me to rethink the whole issue of discipline and to ask, What has happened to school discipline? Perhaps more important is the question, What can a teacher do to effectively discipline his or her class, or even to survive in the classroom today?

Teachers today are faced with some kids that challenge every authority, that test a teacher's resolve in ways that were unimaginable even 15 years ago. I refer to these students as *in-your-face kids*—those who constantly demand attention, most frequently in nonproductive ways. Sometimes it seems as if they dominate the attention of the teacher, even though they may comprise only a small percentage of the class.

This book presents a practical guide for disciplining in-your-face kids, by rethinking the disciplinary issue from the ground up, and presenting practical, proven strategies in a user-friendly manner. The book is also intended as a practical survival guide, which presents strategies that work and that are solidly based in the efficacy research. However, single disciplinary strategies alone will not make any teacher or parent more effective when dealing with children who constantly challenge authority. Rather, an overall reconceptualization of one's disciplinary perspective is required in order to develop a new model into which various strategies fit. This new

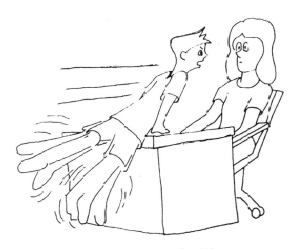

*An in-your-face kid*

construct should assist the teacher or parent in selecting a disciplinary tactic or strategy that is appropriate for a particular child or adolescent at a particular time and in a particular situation.

More than merely presenting another cookbook approach to discipline, this book challenges many of the old-guard strategies and thinking about discipline. Behavioral approaches, which have provided the background for almost every disciplinary program developed for the last 20 years (e.g., Cantor's assertive discipline, Albert's cooperative discipline, and Curwin and Mendler's discipline with dignity), are discussed within the context of a larger disciplinary picture—that is, the crucial issue of the relationship between the teacher and the student. This relationship forms the context of and the basis for all disciplinary interactions within the classroom. Although particular tactics are critical, each strategy should be used only within a broader understanding of how it may impact the pupil/teacher relationship—thus the term *relational discipline.*

Relational discipline focuses squarely on the relationship between the teacher and the student, and various tactics and strategies are implemented within that broader context. For it is this relationship, rather than the specific disciplinary tactics that are used, that forms the basis for appropriate classroom behavior and that eventually develops into self-discipline. This theme will be developed in this chapter and fostered throughout the book.

The book is intended to entertain as well as to teach, so I have taken considerable license and have written very informally. However, teachers are, first and foremost, knowledgeable scholars and practitioners of discipline, and many teachers are conducting action research today in their classrooms. As such, teachers should demand and accept no less than

*Effective teachers build relationships with kids*

research-proven techniques for the classroom. For this reason, the research basis for particular disciplinary tactics is provided in order to demonstrate the efficacy and validity of the specific tactics presented.

> Relational discipline focuses squarely on the relationship between the teacher and the student, and various tactics and strategies are implemented within that broader context.

As a concerned teacher (or parent), you should feel free to sidestep any sections of the book in order to get to the specific suggestions and strategies that you think will work in your classroom. Because the relationships you have established with the students in your class are yours, the disciplinary strategies that you decide to use must be yours also. A strategy that works for someone else may be inappropriate for you, simply because you choose to base your disciplinary relationships on other strategies with which you are more comfortable. On this basis, almost any strategy with research support can be considered as a component of a relational disciplinary plan, but you are the ultimate authority over what tactics you employ. Used in this rather fluid fashion, this book will present you with several ideas about practical methods to handle many disciplinary problems with in-your-face kids. First, we'll take a closer look at the problem of discipline for these kids, and then we'll examine the solutions.

## Are Disciplinary Problems Increasing?

### What Teachers Are Saying

Are disciplinary problems becoming more frequent in schools? The unde-batable answer to that question is yes! For the last two decades, teachers have noticed an increase in discipline problems as well as a decrease in the self-discipline of students at almost every age and grade level. Let me relate a story shared by an experienced teacher with 75 other teachers in a work-shop I conducted in 1999 on discipline:

> I've been a teacher for 16 years, and I've enjoyed every one of those years. I've taught kids from grade 6 down to kindergarten, and I've been teaching kindergarten now for 6 years. But this year, I've got a real problem. Of the 20 kids in my class, 15 are real behavior problems. Seven have IEPs [individualized education

plans] and four others are on Ritalin. I've told the principal that no learning is taking place and that I will need more help to include these kids in my class, but he doesn't have any help to offer. For the first time, I'm not enjoying my teaching—I dread going to school each day. One day last week, I went to the office at noon and told them I was going to go home. I just don't want to do this anymore.

I wish I could state that this was an isolated incident, but unfortunately I hear this type of example every time I conduct a workshop or teach a class. Clearly, something has changed; something has gone terribly wrong. There is an increase in the disciplinary problems that teachers have to deal with, and teachers are crying out for help. Consequently, this problem translates directly into an increasing loss of very effective teachers—and school districts are having a tough time replacing these valued and experienced educators.

Of course, with the loss of a single experienced teacher, one loses some of the capacity to discipline the in-your-face kids for the entire school. I know of no education professional who would seriously argue that beginning teachers with no experience can discipline students as effectively as experienced teachers. Thus, loss of effective teachers provides a body-blow to the overall disciplinary effort of the school.

For this reason, and a host of others, schools reflect less discipline today than a few years ago, and, according to teachers, the problems seem to be increasing. Further, there is little consensus on what strategies are appropriate and how teachers can maintain effective discipline in their classes. In fact, this increase in disciplinary problems has been discussed so frequently in the media that the litany of "causes" or "reasons for the increase in discipline problems in the school" has been memorized by almost every literate American. You know the list.

### Causes of the Breakdown of Discipline
- Too much television
- Breakdown of the American family
- Violence in the media
- Availability of weapons
- Lack of appropriate male role models
- Changes in society's tolerance for deviance
- Less religious influence
- Breakdown of societal institutions
- Lack of respect for authority figures

Certainly this list could go on forever, and by now, if you are like most educators, you have yawned and said, "So what?" Everybody knows this list, but knowing the causes—if, indeed, these are the causes—doesn't tell the teacher what to do about them. Also, these list items don't show the most worrisome aspect of school discipline today: the increase in school violence.

## Violence in the Schools

Coupled with the increase in disciplinary problems—which theoretically teachers should be able to manage within the classroom—there has been an increase in high-profile crime in and around school campuses. Although the number of school shootings has decreased somewhat recently, the several random school shootings have galvanized the nation. The term *random shooting* may be understood as a situation in which most of the victims are not specifically singled out, but shot merely because they happen to be in the immediate area. Names such as Columbine, Jonesboro, and West Paducah resonate with parents' fears about the safety of their kids at school. One look at the numbers tells a scary tale:

### Statistics on School Violence*
- Crimes committed by juveniles have decreased over the last two decades, but the level of violence in juvenile crime has risen dramatically because guns have replaced fists and switchblades as the weapons of choice.
- Thirty-five percent of teachers surveyed in 1996 indicated that verbal abuse of teachers by students was a serious problem in schools.
- Unlike other violent crimes, juvenile homicide has increased over the last 20 years.
- Juveniles are committing more violent crimes at earlier ages, and many juvenile offenders are third-generation violent offenders.
- In 75 percent of the cases when students attack a teacher, there is some conflict existing prior to the attack that escalates. The majority of these attacks do not come "out of nowhere."
- Thirty-four percent of teachers see physical conflicts among students as a serious problem today, compared with only 18 percent in 1987–88.
- Gang violence is a growing problem for inner-city schools, but it accounts for only a small percentage of violence on school campuses.

*These statistics have been compiled from a variety of sources, including Bender and McLaughlin (1997), Sautter (1995), Shen (1997), Stevens (1995), and Walker (1998).

- Violence in inner-city schools is, on the whole, similar in frequency to violence in suburban school districts.

These statistics, like the anecdotes suggesting increasing disciplinary problems in schools, clearly indicate that problems with inappropriate behaviors in schools are increasing. In large measure, this situation leads to other problems in schools, such as teacher burnout, lack of achievement for many students, an increasing number of dropouts, and so on. Recall for a moment the teacher's story related earlier: Will this teacher continue her career in the public school classroom, or is it likely she will seek other employment? The nation hears a great deal of talk about school improvement, national standards, and school reform efforts in the United States today, but no move toward school improvement or school standards will be successful if school discipline problems are not addressed as a major component of the effort. By focusing on relational discipline and attempting to foster the crucial relationship between the teacher and the student, this book will help in the national effort to reform schools in a significant way.

## A New Look at Discipline

### The Old Gods Fail: Beyond Behaviorism

Old gods often fail and leave a feeling of bewilderment. People feel lost and confused, and are unable to understand what has happened. Of course, when old gods fail, they may fail through their own weaknesses or merely because the world changes. Alternatively, the very success of old gods may also lead to their own failure. Behavioral thought—which is the old god in the discipline arena—has served education well for the last three decades, and in many ways has succeeded in assisting to discipline students. However, in this book, I have chosen to challenge the behavioral paradigm, since I believe the "world" of the public school classroom has changed. In these chapters, I have gone beyond the successes of behavioral thought and embraced a broader picture with the relationship between a student and a teacher as the focal point. Thus, I begin by acknowledging both the success and the incomplete nature of behavioral thought.

> Behaviorism is less than effective in public schools because the range of rewards and punishments is so highly limited.

There are several reasons for needing to move beyond behavioral thought. First of all, behavioral practices are often quite cumbersome to implement in the classroom; indeed, some cannot be fully implemented in the public schools today. Specifically, implementation of a full range of highly expensive reinforcements and intrusive punishments is not possible (Walker, 1998) because of the politics of schooling. What teacher wants to use corporal punishment when it can be legally challenged, even in districts where it is still legal? If the authority of parents to use spanking can be legally challenged (as it has been in the courts), such legal challenges are even more likely in the schools. Clearly, public schools can't explore the full range of reward and punishment. Simply put, behaviorism is less than effective in public schools because the range of rewards and punishments that can be administered is so highly limited.

This is particularly true when one considers the types of intrusive punishments that are sometimes used for children with highly self-destructive behaviors. As one example, for children who are autistic and engage in self-mutilation behaviors, a mask that ejects a fine spray of water in the student's face has been used with very positive behavioral results. Of course, this intrusive punishment was legally challenged, in spite of the fact that parents strongly supported the technique because, in many cases, it seemed to be the only strategy that was successful at ending the self-mutilation. (This story made national news several years ago.) Most schools, clearly, would steer away from this type of intrusive punishment, even though it does work.

Likewise, schools cannot typically offer the extreme reinforcement that may be needed by some kids to enhance and assure appropriate behaviors, since the excessive costs for some reinforcement may be prohibitive. In one instance in my own class, I used a new basketball that I purchased as a reward for effective behavior on a behavioral contract. It worked great for the one student I had selected, but I couldn't afford from my teacher's salary at that time to find an appropriate reward of that cost for every student.

Second, teachers should move beyond the rather clinical and disassociated approach that has so often characterized behavioral practice. In many cases, neither the faculty administering a behavioral treatment nor the student recipients are emotionally affected by the treatment. Although offering rewards and/or mild punishments for behaviors can elicit temporary behavioral compliance in a limited number of situations, these treatments work best when the student who is being bribed or punished by the behavioral treatment isn't particularly emotionally involved in the outcome one way or the other. When an in-your-face kid is raging mad, hotheaded, or smoldering in anger, holding that kid in for recess (i.e., a punishment), or offering three minutes of game/activity time contingent on his or her returning to work (i.e., a reinforcement or reward), will usually only make the student more angry.

Walker (1998) considered this problem and concluded that whereas consequences govern trivial behavior, only values can govern critical behavior. In other words, the level of behavioral interventions that are possible in schools today may affect behavior when a student is not emotionally involved, but for more significant behaviors, values or self-discipline are critical. In fact, in most school situations that require the teacher or principal to intervene in a disciplinary fashion, the student is highly emotionally involved, and use of a punishment alone may well invoke a devil-may-care attitude in which the student challenges the teacher to apply more punishment. This type of challenge may be considered a defining characteristic for in-your-face kids. Of course, practicing teachers have long recognized this phenomenon; what good is behavioral theory—or, indeed, any theory on discipline—if the components of it cannot be fully implemented in the classroom?

> Whereas consequences govern trivial behavior, only values can govern critical behavior.

However, Walker's (1998) injunction does stipulate what *does* work: Values can govern critical behavior. Educators need to find ways to understand the motivations of the in-your-face kids who commit overly disruptive behaviors, and seek ways to make those students want to behave differently. In short, teachers need to help restructure these kids' values, and this is possible only through effective relationships between the teacher and the student—the focal point of relational discipline. Ultimately, the focus must become development of self-discipline. Teachers must establish relationships with kids—*all kids*—such that the students themselves want to behave in an appropriate fashion. Only in this manner can discipline, over time, be internalized.

Third, teachers must move beyond behavioral interventions to interventions that can be more readily applied in the classroom. Every educator knows that for all of the talk about behavioral interventions, very few public school teachers have ever applied an educational treatment in a rigorous fashion; the realistic time demands in the typical classroom will not allow for extensive data collection. In fact, few teachers ever collect data in a manner that would be considered appropriate by behavioral scholars. Although token economies are found in many classrooms, very few teachers can present any data charts of students' behavior, and fewer still have implemented a formal behavioral study to demonstrate the efficacy of treatment.

Teachers must move beyond behavioral interventions to interventions that can be more readily applied in the classroom.

Consequently, what one finds passing for behavioral intervention in the schools is, in reality, common sense. Perhaps you are familiar with the use of "Grandma's rule," sometimes expounded in the early behavioral texts: Offer an enjoyable activity after, and contingent on, completion of a difficult activity. That concept has been around for years, and implementation of such a strategy doesn't indicate a wide application of the behavioral theory. Perhaps, in the move both to embrace behavioral practice and to simultaneously move beyond it, teachers should focus on tactics that research has shown to be effective, looking beyond the tactic itself to the likely results it will produce on the relationship between the teacher and the student. Through studious consideration of the relationship, one should be able to find proven tactics that do not require major data-collection efforts and still result in an improved relationship, and consequently an internalization of discipline.

## Why Focus on Relational Discipline?

For most adults, a moment's reflection on our own disciplinary influences from our childhood will help us realize one fundamental tenet of effective discipline. You might vaguely remember a particular reward or punishment you earned during your schooling, but probably what had the most impact on you—indeed, the most significant influence in your memory of

*ADHD nap time*

your own schooling—was the relationship you had with one or more teachers—the relationship you had with the authority figure who was responsible for discipline. Rather than rewards or punishments, you very likely remember the look on the principal's face while you were being scolded, held in from recess, or given detention, or you remember the disappointment and shame you felt when a teacher quietly asked if that was your best work.

> Discipline is a desire to please others and eventually oneself—a desire to be proud of one's behavior and to have the appropriateness of that behavior recognized.

Alternatively, perhaps you remember the care that your teacher showed when he or she held up your class project for special praise, put your written work on the school bulletin board, or assigned you a special responsibility in the classroom. At that moment, you would have jumped through fire for that teacher—and this is what can enlighten you on what discipline really is. Discipline is a desire to please others and eventually oneself—a desire to be proud of one's behavior and to have the appropriateness of that behavior recognized. As a rather personal example, read the following story about a superlative teacher from my own childhood—a tribute I often share in my workshops. This book is dedicated to one of the most effective educators I have ever known: Ms. Julia Whitty.

### A Tribute to Ms. Julia Whitty and Her Kids

Ms. Julia Whitty was, in simple terms, the most effective teacher I ever knew. She taught in a small public school in North Carolina, where she also served as principal. Not only did she make history come alive for me—a passion that still exists in my life—but she also knew how to encourage, to motivate, and to shame (although politically incorrect to say that today, I ask that you withhold judgment until I've provided the example below). In short, she could discipline her class in that rural tobacco-growing town of yesteryear in a way that made small miracles happen each and every year. Of course, that was a different time, and a different world, as far as public schools go, but I do believe that we can, today, learn from excellent teachers in the past.

Ms. Whitty took on all comers, and assigned to her own classroom the hard discipline cases, without exception. For all of her kids, she had one simple imperative: We were to do the best that we could do on each and every task and, by extension, we were to be the best person that we could be. For the sons and daughters of tobacco farmers, those kids needed to learn to read and do math so they could be the best tobacco farmers in the county. For those whose fathers drove a truck or flew a crop duster, all work was related to driving or spraying crops—specifically to help us do our best. For Ms. Whitty, nothing less than the best was ever acceptable, and she routinely gave our assignments back, messy with erasures and corrections, only to request that we recopy correctly for display on her bulletin board of excellence in the school hallway. Every kid in the class had their work on that bulletin board at some point, even if Ms. Whitty had to work with a kid during lunch, recess, or after school to make the end result the best. In my mind, her favorite statement was, "Bill, is that your best work? I'd really like to put that paper up today."

I know of no child that Ms. Whitty taught who did not feel her profound caring, her love for her job as a teacher, and her concern for her kids. We were to be her best, and every child in that small town for two generations experienced that caring. (I should mention that Ms. Whitty also taught my father when he was in the second grade. She knew every family in our small town in that intimate fashion.)

Because she had established such profound relationships with her kids, when it came to discipline, Ms. Whitty merely had to focus on the inappropriate behavior and it would often cease. One look was all it took; perhaps the look was one of displeasure. The shame of the misbehavior dwarfed us all, but it was only a second before Ms. Whitty looked away and changed the subject, sometimes with a question:

"Bill, are you behaving your best?"

"Bill, are you disturbing others?"

"Bill, can you get control of yourself, or should you leave the class?"

In discipline, Ms. Whitty knew to focus on the inappropriate behavior and not the child—and this was long before that tactic became widely understood and recognized. She understood that caring praise, freely and frequently given, was the essential basis of all discipline, and that peers could be profound influences toward either good or bad behavior. Many of the tactics discussed here, including those that have been "proven" by subsequent research, were implemented by Ms. Whitty in the 1940s and

1950s, long before educators were concerned with "proof." In everything she did, her focus was on building relationships with her kids.

In a sense, her profound caring for her students was merely a function of who Ms. Whitty was. She was a servant of her students, first and foremost. While she served as both teacher and principal (thus instructional leader of the school), she saw herself as one whose job it was to get the best from each child in her care. She spent numerous Saturday afternoons (unpaid, of course) opening the school gym so neighborhood kids could play basketball—the three Bender brothers among them. She played the piano every Sunday at the local Baptist church. She gave of herself for bookmobile days and numerous community projects. In doing so, she taught lifelong lessons to generation after generation of kids in that town, and her profound influence can still be felt many years after her death. She disciplined well because she concentrated on relationships with her students—a lesson we can all benefit from today.

At my mother's death from cancer, I'd not seen Ms. Whitty for well over 15 years. Of course, she knew that I was teaching at the University of Georgia. She kept up with every kid from that town for 40 years, and although proud of the numerous tobacco farmers, nurses, auto mechanics, government servants, ministers, doctors, lawyers, and others who had once been her kids, I think she had a special place in her heart for those of us who became teachers. My mom and dad frequently reported that she asked about me, as I'm sure she did all the thousands of kids whose lives had taken them away from that small town.

At one point prior to her death, my mother was sleeping in her hospital bed, and I sat alone with her in the room. My dad and brothers had stepped out for something to eat, and I had begun to cry. Then I heard a soft, so-familiar voice from the door, "How's my Billy doing? Are you still at the University of Georgia? Do you like it there, Bill? Are you writing any more books?" Ms. Whitty, upon her retirement from teaching, had become a volunteer in the local hospital. She and I hugged (she was always big on hugging her kids) and we talked and caught up with each other for a few moments. That was exactly the pick-me-up I needed then, and she stayed with me until my family returned. The love she showed at that critical moment in my life affected me more profoundly than I can ever explain, but it had something to do with continuity and a sense of the completeness of life. That love is enriched by my certainty that she had an impact on hundreds or thousands of her kids in that same deeply personal fashion.

I am a better person for having known Ms. Whitty, and I am a better teacher, having reflected on the subtle lessons she taught. Ms. Whitty could not envision a life in which she did not serve others in some capacity, and she remained in that volunteer position at the hospital until she died. Discipline, for Ms. Whitty, was much more than a set of tactics, approaches, or strategies—it was a relationship of caring, expectations, and hopes yet to be realized. She personified all that was good in education in those days, and my fondest hope for my own career in education is that I can struggle to become the teacher that Ms. Whitty was naturally. In thanks for her caring, her discipline, and her love, this book is a humble tribute.

## What to Keep from Behavioral Thought

> Herein lies a major failure of behavioral thought in education today: ignoring the all-important relationship between the teacher and the student in disciplinary situations.

In an effort to bring psychology into the world of science, behavioral thinkers have, for the most part, overlooked the crucial pupil/teacher relationship as the very foundation for discipline in the schools. Herein lies a major failure of behavioral thought in education today: ignoring the all-important relationship between the teacher and the student in disciplinary situations. Although many behavioral approaches work—and this book will espouse using many of them—the focus in disciplinary efforts today must be on building the exceptionally significant relationship between the teacher and the student. I will build on this relationship theme momentarily, but there are two important aspects of behavioral thought that bear retaining in our disciplinary efforts.

The first of these important aspects is that the accurate measurement of behavioral problems is a major concern in our disciplinary efforts. Although most teachers do not actively measure and chart behaviors, the fact is that teachers would be more effective if they did. Rather than charting behavior to establish scientific validity of one's interventions as recommended by behavioral thought, teachers should chart certain behaviors for one simple reason: Charts are extremely motivating for many kids. Charts of behavioral success can be the basis of an extremely effective disciplinary relationship and may well be a critical aspect of your relational disciplinary plan. The explanation is simple: Charts give the student and the teacher an opportunity to celebrate success—and this builds the all-important relationship.

Whereas the use of charted behavioral problems is effective and should be retained and expanded in public schools, I have the sense that teachers are about ready to "throw the baby out with the bathwater" on this issue. Because behaviorism tends to emphasize the "science" of charting, many teachers fail to recognize the motivational aspects facilitated by charts of performance. In my workshops, when I begin to share strategies that are dependent on charting behaviors, numerous teachers seem to tune out of the discussion. However, charting is important motivationally for many strategies, and the motivational factor allows for building effective relationships. This book will emphasize this theme for certain disciplinary strategies.

With that caution noted, the precision that some behavioral theorists insist on, although useful in scientific journals, is merely a hinderance in the public school classroom and should be abandoned. Use of a standard deceleration chart (e.g., a ratio-based charting format) or a complicated reward structures chart can be very cumbersome, and there is no reason for teachers to be concerned with the full implementation of a behavioral research design for every learning behavior. The complexity of these procedures prevents many teachers from implementing them. For example, what does a teacher do with 25 other kids while charting complex data on the behavior of only one child? Rather, teachers should be focused on teaching, and charting behaviors only in a very limited number of specific incidents, and, in those cases, charting data in a very simplified form. Such a form should be immediately understandable to the child and specifically chosen both to motivate the student and to document the efficacy of treatment.

Alternatively, teachers might teach students to take data on their own behavior, since this can be a very effective behavior-change mechanism. (This is why this concept is used in many adult programs such as Weight Watchers and others.) Such self-charting or self-monitoring can become an important aspect of self-discipline as well as the basis for extensive praise for good performance. Clearly, this practice should be expanded.

One other aspect of behavioral thought should be maintained. Behavioral thought serves the function of focusing educators on the efficacy of various rewards and punishments, and many curricula designs have built successfully on that idea. For example, very few computer-assisted instructional programs would be effective without significant attention to appropriate rewards liberally administered in the electronic environment. Thus, the consideration of motivational factors that are dependent on rewards is crucial to considerations of discipline. Students should be elaborately and frequently praised whenever appropriate.

However, teachers today must think much more broadly than is typical of behavioral scientists. For instance, the following strategies will look at rewards that may be administered "unofficially" by the student's peer group. A great deal can be learned from peer-group interaction about what influences behavior in the social arena. As teachers, we must consider this aspect in our disciplinary efforts.

## Relational Discipline

The realities about discipline in today's schools may be rather worrisome for educators, but moving beyond a narrow focus on behavioral approaches may seem even more frightening. For some, it may be easier to consider relational discipline and the strategies espoused herein as a refinement of behavioral thought. For others, this may seem like an entirely new approach. As the author, my only interest is to focus on the relationship-based aspects of discipline that have so far been largely ignored.

> The disciplinary efforts of any authority figure are successful to the degree that they build on relationships and facilitate further relationships with the students and for the students.

For the title of this book, I borrowed a term from Bill Page, a nationally recognized theorist in education. The entire focus of this book is on *relational discipline*. The disciplinary efforts of any authority figure are successful to the degree that they build on relationships and facilitate further relationships with the students and for the students. Thus, building effective relationships will be the primary organizer for this relational discipline approach. In order to understand the importance of relationships in your disciplinary efforts, note three bases for relational discipline:

1. The student's attention tank
2. Relationships with teachers and mentors
3. Developmental progression to self-discipline

The remainder of this chapter looks at each of these three cornerstones of discipline and shows how schools and society have changed to deemphasize these cornerstones. This discussion provides a background for the specific strategies that follow later in the book.

## Filling the Attention Tank

It should come as no surprise to any teacher or parent that children need attention. In fact, if one listens to parents, one will realize that most children seem to need much more attention than parents can possibly give them, given the parents' work schedules, daily shopping needs, carpooling, health-care appointments, and other home-management responsibilities. It is extremely difficult for most parents to give their own children the attention they need and deserve. In fact, the most certain way to elicit guilt on the part of almost any parent is to inquire how much time the parent spends with his or her kids.

Of course, if this is true at home, it is even more true at school. The need for attention, which is a need every student has, in the typical school classroom is multiplied by a factor of 25 or 30 (i.e., the number of kids in that classroom). As opposed to 1, 2, or 3 children in the average home, teachers have 20 to 30 in the average school class. A secondary teacher may have 120 to 150 students in his or her class daily, and each of those students has different needs for attention and different methods for getting those needs met. In fact, 10 to 25 percent of these students may be considered in-your-face kids, demanding much more attention than the others. Based on these numbers, it is reasonable to wonder how any teacher can hope to give each and every student in a typical school classroom the attention he or she needs.

> Think of students as giant attention tanks—similar to gas tanks on cars—that need to be filled every so often with attention.

Perhaps because of my work with students with learning disabilities and/or attention deficit disorders, I have begun to think of students as giant attention tanks—similar to gas tanks on cars—that need to be filled every so often with attention. To my knowledge, Mr. Ron Walker, a former teacher and school administrator, was the first to use this metaphor (Walker, 1998). This is quite understandable, since Mr. Walker specialized in students with learning disabilities and attention deficit disorders also.

*Different sizes of attention tanks*

Using this analogy, one of the primary realities of the classroom is that all students have attention tanks; some kids have very small attention tanks, some kids have medium-sized attention tanks, and some kids have very large attention tanks. Furthermore, all students will get their attention tanks filled whenever they need to; that is, *they will get the attention they need in whatever manner seems to work for them.*

Of course, teachers relate well to students with small attention tanks. Most educators with classroom experience can think of kids who could be classified as relatively "low maintenance"—that is, students who make few demands on the teacher's time, who generally get their work done on time, and so on. Alternatively, all teachers have had experience with students with very large attention tanks—those who are excessively "clingy," who won't let go of the teacher's sleeve, and who seem to need attention all the time. Most teachers, upon reading this statement, can immediately picture one or two students in the class like this.

Those with large attention tanks may also be the students who entertain the class (either in positive or negative ways), who create social problems in the classroom, and who create disciplinary problems merely to amuse their peers. These students tend to be the class clowns or the class bullies.

> Every student is an attention tank, and every student will have his or her attention tank filled! You cannot put off filling a tank that demands attention, nor can you ignore the attention needs of that student or the others in the class.

The fact is, there is a wide variety of ways to get one's attention needs met; unfortunately, many of these ways are highly disruptive of the routine in the public school classroom. All teachers have had a sense of *deja vu* when dealing with a disciplinary problem, because it's often the very same disciplinary problem that they dealt with from the same student last week, yesterday, or five minutes ago! Remember, every student is an attention tank, and every student will have his or her attention tank filled! As a teacher, you cannot put off filling a tank that demands attention, nor can you ignore the attention needs of that student or the others in the class. The 25 to 30 attention tanks will be filled one way or the other, and you may as well organize your day and your class to meet these diverse needs. In fact, your day *will be* organized around meeting these needs, whether you like it or not. Naturally, it will be more effective if you plan to meet these needs in advance, based on your knowledge of what levels of attention each student needs.

> Students, not teachers, will determine what *kind* of attention fills their tanks.

Another subtle rule to remember about attention tanks is that students, not teachers, will determine what *kind* of attention fills their tanks. As a teacher, you may think that increasing your praise for little Billy Bender's math work will give Billy the attention he needs. While this is one option, and praise frequently given is one mark of an effective teacher, Billy may not want or respond to your praise. Billy may decide that he wants his positive attention from the little girl across the aisle and/or his peers in the class, rather than from you. Consequently, only through entertaining the class with his rapier wit and/or his clown-like behavior will Billy's attention tank be filled. In fact, praise from you—the teacher—may be the opposite of what Billy wants, since that may suggest that he is a "teacher's pet," and Billy certainly doesn't want to suggest that view to the little girl across the aisle. Billy may intentionally act up immediately after praise, since he then has to reestablish his credentials as the class clown! In fact, he may also bully other kids to show what a "man" he is, now that he is a grown-up fourth-grader.

The attention tank phenomenon, then, is one organizing principle of relational discipline. In some ways, this may be considered a layperson's refinement of Maslow's hierarchy of needs. For those of you so inclined, one intellectual exercise you might enjoy would be to overlay the attention tank concept on Maslow's hierarchy, and see what thoughts that picture brings to mind.

> The single-biggest cause of discipline problems in the nation's schools may be anonymity.

If the attention tank metaphor is valid, then the single-biggest cause of disciplinary problems in today's schools may not be violence on television, inappropriate role models, the breakdown of the family, or any of the other "causes" typically espoused. Rather, the single-biggest cause of discipline problems in the nation's schools may be anonymity. In other contexts (Bender, 1999), I have used the phrase *invisible kids* to represent the kids in schools who, although not overt discipline problems, may occasionally demonstrate very disruptive or even violent behavior. When students today feel invisible in school—that is, when their attention tanks are empty—they feel that nobody really knows or cares who they are. In extreme cases, their desire for some attention will rule out common sense and even rationality. And therein lies a large part of the problem of discipline in schools today—kids are demanding attention, many times in frightening ways. The recent examples of overt violence in schools in Littleton, West Paducah, Columbine, and Jonesboro have been interpreted by the national media as a desire for attention by many of the perpetrators (Shubert, Bressette, Deeken, & Bender, 1999)—hence the term *invisible kids.*

In fact, all students need avenues by which they can receive positive attention for appropriate behavior, and schools are not filling that need. Further, as presently structured, schools cannot fill that need for every student. Unfortunately, schools today are less well equipped than schools of yesteryear to provide for the attention needs of the students for a variety of reasons.

One of those reasons is that schools in the 1960s and 1970s tended to be much smaller than schools of today. It is not uncommon today to find high schools in large suburban areas of well over 2,500 or even 3,000 students. Even very large elementary schools are becoming the norm rather than the exception, and in terms of meeting the attention needs of students, this is clearly the wrong way to go.

McPartland, Jordan, Legters, and Balfanz (1997) recognized this "anonymity" problem in a large high school in Baltimore. The school had a student population from an inner-city area of over 2,000—largely unmotivated—students. These authors assisted in the restructuring of that school into smaller "academies" that focused on particular curricular areas and emphasized the contributions of every student. By delineating different "schools within a school," the teachers in that large high school were able to give almost every student a meaningful role, and thus fill each student's attention tank. As these authors reported, the change in that school has been phenomenal! Students have begun to feel connected to their teachers, their peers, and their school in a new and profound way. This, again, points to the overriding importance of the attention tank phenomenon in a teacher's disciplinary efforts. Now let's look at one method for meeting the attention tank needs of students through the use of others.

## Relationships: The Key to Effective Discipline

> In situations where students are not known by name, one does not have discipline in any meaningful sense.

Relational discipline is founded on the overriding importance of building a relationship between the student and the teacher or another authority figure in the school environment. As long as students are anonymous in schools, very little can be done to facilitate effective discipline. In situations where students are not known by name, one does not have discipline in any meaningful sense. All one can realistically hope for in those situations is effective policing and/or crowd control.

### How We Got Here

One may well ask, How were the nation's schools transformed from educational institutions into institutions that spend substantial time policing students' behavior? One answer to this question has already been discussed: The sheer numbers of students alone prohibit teachers from providing meaningful, in-depth, personal relationships with every student. However, in addition to building larger schools, another answer lies in the fact that schools have been restructured in some problematic ways. Consider, as one example, the direction of U.S. schools during the last five decades.

In the 1950s, it was quite common for students up through eighth grade (i.e., into and through puberty) to have only one teacher, who taught every subject in the curriculum. Of course, that teacher, although not a content expert in each and every subject, did have intimate insight and understanding of every individual child in the class. Granted, in-depth mentoring was not possible (one adult can never adequately serve as mentor to 30 kids), still the fact is that the teacher at least knew every student quite well.

At that point, even high schools tended to be small, one-town affairs, and teachers in grades 9 through 12 lived in the same neighborhood as most of their students. All of these factors made for more intimate and meaningful personal relationships between pupils and teachers, and fostered mentor-type relationships throughout the school.

However, in the 1950s and 1960s, the United States witnessed a consolidation movement for high schools, based on the belief that math and science classes, in particular, could be taught more effectively by consolidating smaller high schools into larger schools with expensive science labs. These were the days of *Sputnik*—the days of a reactionary wake-up call that the nation was lagging in the field of education. A heavy emphasis was placed on science by building bigger schools with state-of-the-art laboratory facilities and training teachers to be content-area specialists in science. Students changed classes and went to various teachers who were content experts in numerous subjects. Of course, this movement toward larger schools then shifted to the lower grades, with the junior high movement occurring in the 1970s and the subsequent middle school movement in the 1980s. Today, it is not uncommon to have fourth-graders changing classes and being taught by four or five teachers a day.

*"Billy, you are not blind, and that
is not a seeing eye frog!"*

What people didn't realize during this evolution in schools is that moving into departmentalized schools with students changing classes in lower-level grades tends to break down the critical relationship between a pupil and a teacher—one of the most important aspects of education. When a teacher teaches 30 students for a full day, that teacher will, of necessity, know those students intimately; that is not the case when the teacher instructs 60 to 120 students a day. If one believes, as I do, that the pupil/teacher relationship is the single-most important variable in discipline, affecting students' behavior as well as their long-term social development, then one must conclude that the move toward content-certified teachers and departmentalized curriculum in the lower grades has been a disaster to education in the United States for many students. Clearly, no fourth-grade history/language arts teacher who works with 80 or 100 students in four blocks each day will know all of those students well. As a result, the critical aspect of effective education—the pupil/teacher relationship—suffers pitifully.

### *Can Teachers Be Mentors?*

Effective mentoring challenges the participants to behave in a certain fashion, and this requires a high level of intimacy and a significant time commitment.

Prior to school consolidation and departmentalized curricula, teachers had 25 to 30 kids, and intimate mentoring even then could not and did not take place for each of those kids by a teacher. Effective mentoring is a very personal relationship that challenges the participants to behave in a certain fashion, and this requires a high level of intimacy and a significant time commitment. Thus, although teachers who teach 25 students all day do have a better chance of meeting many of the attention tank needs for their kids, those teachers will still not be able to mentor each of those students effectively. Mentoring must be seen as much more involved than merely meeting the students' attention needs. It requires even smaller numbers and more personal relationships between adults and students.

Of course, neither the attention tank needs nor the mentoring needs will be met in today's massive departmentalized schools. The nation's schools need to establish more programs such as the Baltimore example, in which students are allowed and encouraged to "shine" in small groups (see Chapter 4).

In fact, at some point, schools may wish to conceptualize a unique type of secondary school, which I refer to as a *developmental high school*. As an intellectual exercise (rather than as a concept I actively advocate), I challenge my graduate students occasionally with the following example: Imagine a primary, elementary, and secondary school district in which, up through grade 10 or so, one teacher teaches 25 students every subject in the curriculum. In that imaginary context, the teacher would know each of those students intimately and would develop a better understanding of each child's emotional and/or attention tank needs. Of course, there may need to be some separation after grade 10 in vocational and college-prep areas, but, as a certified secondary teacher, I believe that good teachers have the ability to teach every subject in the curriculum effectively, up through algebra II, a couple of history classes, English classes, literature classes, civics, and so on—in other words, the usual first two years of high school.

In that imaginary school, the teacher would have 22 to 28 students that he or she knew extremely well and could serve as a mentor for a number of them. My hypothesis is that disciplinary problems would decrease substantially and that more effective pupil/teacher relationships would occur at higher grade levels.

This concept, of course, is heresy for many educators, who have built their careers attempting to become content experts in various subject areas. In fact, most teacher unions and professional organizations today are so dedicated to certification by content area that even this suggestion for reform may draw sharp criticism. Clearly, such a drastic change would represent an experiment in real school reform and would need to be carefully conceptualized. Still, this may be a direction that some experimental school should consider: Is anyone out there up for an interesting challenge?

### The Need for Mentors

Mentoring approaches offer the possibility of an appropriate adult role model filling a kid's attention tank.

Given the current structure for middle, junior high, and secondary schools, educators need to provide other avenues for students to establish meaningful relationships that encourage appropriate behavioral role modeling. For this reason, many researchers are beginning to attend to the concept of mentoring. Mentoring approaches offer the possibility of an appropriate adult role model filling a kid's attention tank. Research on mentoring has demonstrated the overall efficacy of this approach (Gottfredson, 1998).

Consider for a moment the list of causes of discipline problems cited earlier and notice the number of examples that have to do with relationships (lack of a male/female role model in home or school, breakdown of the family, etc.). Does this reveal something about discipline that we have been missing? Consider, also, the "laboratory" of one's own experiences, one's own memories. Often, in my workshops I invite the teachers or parents to reflect on their childhoods and some of the "trouble spots" or "bad spots" they experienced during their youth. I then ask those adults to share why they were embarrassed by that experience and how they managed at that time to get through such a tough time. In most cases, the responses I get to these inquiries have to do with a desire to live up to the expectations of some significant adult in their lives (e.g., a parent, a grandparent, a teacher, a minister, an older brother or sister, or almost any other adult role model). Clearly, mentors have a significant and profound impact on a person's behavior, and clearly it would be wise to consider a very structured approach to providing mentoring for every in-your-face kid in school.

For this reason, another relational disciplinary theme involves the application of mentoring strategies for discipline. What is needed by many children is an effective relationship with a significant adult—a mentor that the child can look up to, can respect, and wishes to emulate. In fact, in many ways, a mentor relates to a young adolescent much like a peer—making suggestions, serving as a sounding board for problems, listening attentively, and so on. In other ways, the mentor clearly serves as an adult role model. Many kids' emotional needs can be significantly fulfilled only by such a multifaceted relationship.

> Many schools are structuring plans to bring in community mentors, with the specific goal of pairing these mentors with the students at risk for behavioral problems.

Puberty and the years immediately after puberty are typically the most effective time for a mentorship relationship. Mentors are usually adults from the community who can encourage, cajole, discuss, and generally influence these young adolescents. In fact, many schools are structuring plans to bring in community mentors, with the specific goals of pairing these mentors with the students at risk for behavioral problems (Clinton & Miles, 1999). Mentors, rather than parents or even teachers, can usually be much more effective at encouraging students to make appropriate choices about various issues. It is for this reason that numerous societies have institutionalized a mentorship approach to child rearing.

> It is a terrible mistake for today's society to have no structured rituals or systematic way to assist young men and women in finding their roles in society.

One often-cited example is that of Native Americans in the midwestern plains. In that society, at the age of 12 to 14, young males were paired with an "uncle" who was a warrior in the tribe. Any male warrior in the tribe, other than the father, could serve as the uncle (or mentor) for the young male. This uncle would arrange for the young male to find ways to demonstrate his bravery, or skill, in hunting, running, and fighting (i.e., all survival skills for the tribe). He would also help interpret the dreams of the boy in an effort to assist the young man in determining his place in that society, his contribution to the tribe. This mentorship phase in development of the young man's life was not only seen as a critical phase for him but also for the tribe. It was during this phase that the young man cemented his relationship with his larger society, and thereby found his place as a contributing member of the tribe. Today, U.S. society would do quite well to emulate this example. I believe that it is a terrible mistake for today's society to have no structured rituals or systematic way to assist young men and women in finding their roles in society.

Some organized structures do exist for obtaining mentors for certain students. For many adolescents, this type of mentoring is found in organized sports, in church or synagogue relationships, and in community activities, and those youngsters tend to be the least likely to demonstrate repeated behavioral problems in school. The adolescents who are not involved in sports, band, after-school extracurricular activities, and so on tend to be the students who repeatedly cross the principal's threshold for disciplinary reasons, and it is these students who most need some type of mentoring.

One interesting note: For overt offenders—the hard-core violent kids—mentoring is taking place. However, it is not the type of mentoring society wants. For example, one of the most common methods for mentoring young African American, Hispanic American, and Caucasian males from the inner-city involves gang membership. Many young males are exceptionally socialized to the requirements of their local gang's rules and obligations, and generally look to gang leaders as their mentors—a dubious source for information on what appropriate adult behavior is. Clearly, adolescents who are even partially socialized to the gang will need a great deal of attention to wean them away from this unwholesome gang influence, and very few programs have been shown to be effective in this regard.

The good news is that more and more agencies in society are realizing this need for structured mentorships based in the schools or community. Agencies such as Big Brother and Big Sister, and programs such as 100 Black Men of Atlanta provide effective mentoring models; even the Lions International Organization has a mentoring program. These types of programs can be the most effective disciplinary intervention for many kids with behavioral problems (Gottfredson, 1998). Information on creating mentorships is becoming more available to educators (see further discussion in Chapter 3), and I recommend that educators initiate efforts to form mentorships in their local schools.

## The Developmental Progression to Self-Discipline

### Why a Developmental Perspective?

Total agreement on effective disciplinary ideas is rare, but there is general agreement on the desire to have all students develop self-discipline. Even the behavioral theorists made some rudimentary efforts at "generalization to other behavioral settings" (i.e., discipline that originates with the student), and almost every disciplinary system developed since the 1970s emphasized some type of self-discipline.

However, beyond this general agreement on the desire for self-discipline, few theorists care to tread. I'm reminded of the fifteenth-century maps of the world showing only Europe, Asia Minor, and parts of Africa. In the Atlantic, since nobody knew what an ocean really was or what was across it, mapmakers drew whales and monsters, and issued the stern warning: *"Don't Go! Here be whales and monsters!"*

> Ignorance of how to accomplish a task leads to relatively few attempts at the task.

In other words, ignorance of how to accomplish a task leads to relatively few attempts at the task. Too often, in considerations of certain aspects involved in discipline in schools (e.g., male role models in the classroom), teachers fear to tread—"Here be whales and monsters!" Still, if one applies a relational perspective to one's understanding of disciplinary issues, this will lead to a focus on the development of self-discipline and its relationship to earlier forms of discipline.

As an aside, it is interesting to note that while almost every aspect of the nation's educational endeavor has been dissected and studied by developmental psychologists (e.g., reading growth across the age span, language development, cognitive development, written language, moral development, sexual/social development, etc.), the primary theorists in discipline provide almost no discussion from a developmental perspective of discipline across the middle and secondary school years. It makes one wonder, How did we educators miss that? Perhaps more important is the question,

Where can the concept of development of discipline over the childhood and young adult years lead us? Again—beware of the whales and monsters!

### Adult-Imposed Discipline

Clearly, young children start out as relatively undisciplined beings who respond to disciplinary interventions in much the same fashion as any other animal capable of learning. Thus, behavioral thought regarding rewards and punishments is "correct" in that all learning beings do learn from a combination of reinforcement and punishments. However, human animals are impacted by a number of additional factors, such as language, personality, socialization, and a desire to please one's peers and oneself. Further, it is hoped that discipline is internalized by each child and that all children become relatively independent-minded adults. Clearly, society must attend more concretely to this shift in the origination of discipline; in fact, people should do everything they can to facilitate it.

During the early years of childhood, a child has very little internal discipline. A wide variety of behavioral strategies (reward, punishment, etc.) work for young children and continue to work for older children. Numerous disciplinary systems have been built around these approaches (the STEP program, assertive discipline, etc.), and almost all of these programs can present some evidence that they work. In fact, I recommend many of these programs for teachers and/or parents who have specific problems with children in their care.

Still, most of these programs are incomplete in that they do not consider the relationship between the individuals involved in discipline nor the continuing development of self-discipline in the child. When the disciplinary effectiveness of the adult world declines—beginning at about the time of puberty—what replaces it? We'll get back to that question a little later.

Note that this developmental concept of discipline postulates that initial discipline is imposed on the young child by others. The parents are the first disciplinarians, and teachers eventually share that parental role in the sense that both parents and teachers represent adults that impose discipline on the young child. Behavioral interventions can be quite effective at this stage, since compliance, rather than true disciplinary understanding, is a major goal (at least for very young children who may not be cognitively developed enough to master a complex cause-and-effect sequence). Have you ever had the experience of watching a parent attempt to "explain" a disciplinary issue to a child who was obviously much too young to understand the parent's reasoning? Experts in discipline clearly have done certain parents no good at all, when long, drawn-out verbal explanations of cause and effect are offered to a child of 18 months. Most children at that age are simply too young to understand such explanations, and yet some parents feel that providing detailed explanations in that fashion is the mark of a truly loving parent.

> Effective parental discipline, then, is one of the best predictors of which children will manifest appropriate or inappropriate behavior in school.

Still, parents are the first disciplinarians, and many disciplinary instances are handled by young couples who are just beginning to understand how to be parents. Parents begin to discipline their child on the first day of life, through facial expressions, sighs of exasperation, and numerous other nonverbal communication mechanisms. Thus, parental discipline is a forerunner of discipline in the school and of self-discipline throughout life. Effective parental discipline, then, is one of the best predictors of which children will manifest appropriate or inappropriate behavior in school.

This outside-imposed discipline, however, works only for a short while in the life of the child. In fact, one corollary of this relational view of discipline is the essential need to build a disciplinary system that progresses far beyond adult-imposed discipline and that moves eventually to self-discipline. This principle is one of the major shortcomings of behavioral thought since, try as they might, behaviorists never managed to move into self-discipline instruction with the same vigor that they moved into, say, behavioral measurement. Often, parents as well as teachers get stuck in the rut of thinking that they "discipline" a 14-year-old child in the same fashion that they discipline a 6-year-old child. In fact, neither behavioral thought nor most of the currently available disciplinary systems (e.g., assertive discipline, discipline with dignity, etc.) makes any differentiation for tactics used at different ages, and this is clearly a mistake.

As one final thought on the adult-imposed phase of discipline, we must consider the attention tank phenomenon. Recall that the golden rule of attention tanks is that the tanks must be filled. Clearly, when adults are the primary disciplinary influence in kids' lives, the adults must fill the tanks. For instance, young children can often entertain each other for a brief while, but every parent can recall the need of children to play immediately under the feet of the adults, rather than play with peers in another room. This is because, at that stage, only communication and attention from adults can fill young children's attention tanks. Also, teachers of young children can recall many children who always pulled teachers' sleeves—until the teachers' clothes were in utter disarray—simply to get attention! In summary, during the adult-imposed discipline phase, adults must take the lion's share of responsibility for filling children's attention tanks.

### Who's Up?

Of course, at some point, the imposed discipline from the adult world loses much of its effectiveness; in other words, adults are no longer able to fill the children's attention tanks. Many parents and teachers are surprised at how quickly this change takes place—it seems, with certain children, to be almost overnight! However, the question arises, When the influence of adults begins to wane in a child's life, what replaces it?

> Are hormones exclusively to blame for the insanity of family life, or do kids merely go crazy for a few years?

Remember the questions from the softball diamonds of your youth: Who's up? Who's up to bat? Whose turn is it now? This is the best way to understand the first major progression of discipline—the question of who's up next in the ultimate progression of disciplinary influences. What, specifically, replaces the discipline imposed on the child by the adults in the environment? What happens to kids when they hit puberty and the young adolescent years? Are hormones exclusively to blame for the insanity of family life, or do these kids merely go crazy for a few years? The answer to these questions is apparent when one steps back and takes a good look at the growing youngsters themselves. Consider the following questions:

- Do kids at age 11, 12, or 13 choose to dress like their parents?
- Who do 12-year-old kids want to walk with in the mall?
- Do kids' hairstyles reflect those of the adult world?
- Who are kids in early adolescence interested in being like?
- Who do kids hang out with?
- Who do these kids dress like?

> To know who influences youngsters at puberty, merely watch the kids interact with their peers!

The answer to all of these questions points directly to one of the major disciplinary influences in the life of the young adolescent: the peer group.

To know who influences youngsters at puberty, merely watch the kids interact with their peers! As the time spent with parents and family declines (as it does in the life of almost every young adolescent, from the age of 11 or 12 on up), peers begin to gain influence in the life of almost every kid. This represents the early peer influence period. During these years, most kids eat like their peers; dress like their peers; use make-up and jewelry like their peers; cut their hair like their peers; and absolutely must have the same style of shoes, pants, dresses, sweaters, bathing suits, shirts, hats, and so on as their peers. The last thing that any 13-year-old kid would be caught dead doing is walking through the mall with his or her parents.

> Parents are clearly a social disease that most 13-year-olds consider to be quite contagious.

Now, this is no great surprise to any parent of older youngsters, nor to any teacher who has taught kids from the fifth grade and higher. Most adults know that young adolescents—while not exactly despising adults—are very much less inclined to want to be seen with adults in public. In the view of the young adolescent, parents are clearly a social disease that most 13-year-olds consider to be quite contagious. What parent hasn't felt confused or even somewhat unloved by his or her young teenager, and rationalized that feeling by thinking, "He (or she) is just growing up!" There is clearly no surprise here; peers are at this point a major influence on discipline—perhaps the most significant influence on behavior overall.

What is surprising—*startling* would be a better word—is the fact that few disciplinary systems have, in any comprehensive manner, chosen to build on the influence of the peer group in disciplining students in the middle school, junior high, or high school. With all the collective insight, experience, and intelligence of all the teachers, principals, college faculty, and psychologists who make a living off disciplinary concerns, I must ask again, How did we miss that?

Although the influence of the peer group begins much earlier, it is not until and after puberty that the importance of this influence begins to rival the influence of parents and teachers. As students start to awaken sexually (i.e., during and toward the end of Freud's latency stage of sexual development), they begin to attend rather dramatically to their peers. Males begin to "strut their stuff" blatantly and females begin to primp to attract the attentions of males. In fact, at this point, both "strutting one's stuff" and "primping" become significant social bonding activities. Males begin to perform their adolescent sexual displays together (e.g., two junior high boys walk together to get a soft drink during the basketball game) and females begin to primp collectively in the bathroom, sometimes for many hours at a time. Further, this is the age at which it is socially acceptable to have a boyfriend or girlfriend; the importance of sexual attraction during this period is overwhelming.

Teachers and parents sense that their influence on kids' lives is decreasing during these years, and this often causes some regret. Note that their influence does not disappear entirely; it merely wanes. This typically happens at some point during the middle grades, and by the junior high grades, most kids seem completely otherworldly, causing parents to scratch their heads and say to themselves, "Where did she (or he) get that from?"

> Adolescents need the attention of other adolescents, and if teachers can harness the power of this social attention need, many disciplinary problems will be quickly solved.

For this reason, teachers need to consider disciplinary strategies that offer youngsters the kinds of attention that the kids feel they need. The attention tank problem is still present, but it is manifested in a different way. Adolescents need the attention of other adolescents, and if teachers can realize this and harness the power of this social attention need, which is the driving need for most young adolescents, many disciplinary problems will be quickly solved.

Any disciplinary system that focuses on relationships must look to a variety of disciplinary strategies that utilize and impact the relationships within the peer group as well as the person(s) manifesting the behavioral problem. Here, the "relational" aspect of relational discipline must involve the relationship with peers in addition to the relationship with teachers or mentors. Strategies that use the energy of the peer group to effect positive change in behavior must be included in every middle grade teacher's arsenal of strategies. Numerous tactics of this nature are presented in this book, and you should choose several that feel comfortable for you.

### Move into Self-Discipline

After the peer influence period, most students move into a self-discipline period in which they formulate behavioral expectations for themselves. Having students make this final disciplinary transition to self-discipline should be every teacher's overriding disciplinary goal.

Concerning disciplinary matters, all parents and teachers share the goal of hoping that the child will eventually grow into a self-reliant person—a person who makes his or her own choices, who is fully cognizant of the consequences of those choices, and who takes responsibility for those choices. After all, this is part of what it means to be an adult, and having some degree of self-love and self- respect is essential here. Educators need to intentionally structure school activities that allow every student to "shine," because shining one's light is the manner in which people learn to value themselves. Also, herein lies one of the single-largest failures of many educational endeavors. One simple example will illustrate this point.

In my consultant work with parents of children with ADHD, learning disabilities, or behavioral disorders, I repeatedly ask about what hobbies or activities the parents could assist the child to build into his or her life that would allow the child to display a unique talent or knowledge that would make the kid someone special. I typically mention karate, sports, musical talent, go-cart driving, flying, dancing, and so on. For example, students as young as age 13 can begin the study for a pilot's license. Imagine what a major ego boost this would be for almost any student—he or she can do something no other kid in class can do, and therein lie certain bragging rights!

> Development of a special hobby, talent, or capability will enhance self-esteem and lead to self-disciplined behavior all around.

A personal note is relevant here. When I was 9 years old, I liberated (or stole) an unused guitar from my younger brother's closet, and began to try to tune it. I asked my Uncle Van Bender (one of several mentors) to show me some guitar chords. My parents noticed this, and for Christmas that year, I got a cheap guitar and subsequently learned to play. In many ways, that has been a defining moment in my life; I played at parties and pizza joints in high school and college, and was in a number of bands. Even today, many years later, on a sunny summer Sunday afternoon, one can frequently find me with an old Martin six string in some cornfield in the Southeast playing bluegrass with several thousand other country music fans. My Mom and Dad gave me a hobby that stuck for life, and thus created not only high self-esteem in at least one area of my life during those critical puberty years but also numerous opportunities for interesting social options later on. It was neat to be the kid in high school that everyone knew as a good guitarist and singer. I can never repay my Mom and Dad for that careful watchfulness, and I hope over time to do as well with my own son. Development of a special hobby, talent, or capability will enhance self-esteem and lead to self-disciplined behavior all around.

The transition to self-discipline typically happens in secondary school, and part of this transition to self-reliance on disciplinary matters is the reduction of the influence of the peer group, in lieu of increasing self-initiated discipline. In other words, most all parents hope that their child will learn to "just say no" to drugs, early sex, drinking and driving, and so on at some point during high school, even if all the kid's peers seem to be "doing it." This discipline, then, reflects a self-imposed disciplinary standard, and the ultimate goal of any disciplinary plan must be to move a student into this type of self-discipline.

Parents and teachers can and do have a very profound impact on discipline, even during middle to late adolescence; the recent national study of adolescent health and safety by Resnick and his colleagues (1997) emphasized the importance of the parental influence even during late adolescence. Remember, though, that this influence is not exercised in the same fashion as the earlier adult-imposed discipline; the disciplinary tactics of both parents and teachers must change during this later phase. For the first seven or so years of life, size difference is one factor impacting disciplinary influences (i.e., the adult is physically bigger); during the teenage years, however, adults must use other strategies. Specifically, adults must reason with adolescents and hope to convince the youngsters of the adults' perspective—one adult to another. At this point, the disciplinary influence is predominately relationally based and deals with gentle guidance, persuasion, and subtle influence rather than harsh rule-based behavior and overt rewards and punishments.

This is why many disciplinary plans for early childhood discipline emphasize choices for children. They represent an attempt to get children thinking about making decisions based on their decision-making prowess. Although a number of parent training programs have emphasized this, the concept of choices has been only tentatively applied in public school classes. Also, emphasis on child choices during the developmental level, when peers have a major emphasis on discipline, may not be appropriate. Do you remember how strong your desires were during early adolescence? Making choices on that basis shouldn't be regarded as the definitive disciplinary model.

## Putting It All Together: The Relational Discipline Model

Figure 1.1 depicts the elements of relational discipline by emphasizing the relationships that have an impact on discipline. The time element illustrates the differential influences on the discipline of the child over time. Again,

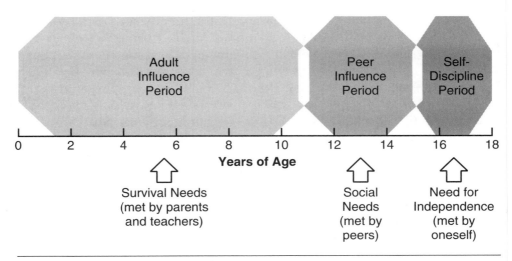

**FIGURE 1.1** *Relational Discipline*

this is intended to display only the predominate influence on the child's behavior, not the only influences on behavior during any phase of a child's life. For example, even during the adult-imposed discipline phase prior to the age of 10, peers can and do influence discipline to some degree. In fact, the peer-group influence begins to grow when students begin formal schooling, but the real growth of peer influence begins immediately after puberty. Further, both adults and peers continue to influence discipline well into the adult years of self-imposed discipline. Of course, in addition to these multiple influences, many adults and/or peers may be affecting a child's behavior at any one time; most of these influences will be positive, but some may be less than desirable. The positive influences may include parents, teachers, Sunday School teachers, coaches, band directors, and other instructors of extracurricular activities, whereas the less desirable influences may include a neighborhood gang, a drug dealer at school, a boyfriend or girlfriend, and a peer who behaves inappropriately.

Still, the predominate influences are shown in the model in the general order in which they begin to significantly affect a child's behavior. Just prior to and during puberty, peers begin to exercise an inordinate amount of influence. These are the years when parents are largely ignored as a primary influence. Subsequently, by the early high school years, some degree of self-discipline should be evident.

The term *mentoring* could be superimposed over the peer influence period in this model. This is because mentors can, and often do, have influence during that period when the traditional parental influence is waning. Mentors may be teachers or others who have a significant impact on the child's behavior during the peer influence phase and afterward. For a number of reasons, mentors are more effective during these later years, though mentorships can be effective at any time. Many mentorship programs begin around the fifth grade or so and continue into and through secondary school. Unfortunately, although mentoring programs are supported by research (Gottfredson, 1998), mentors are not routinely available for many children, and some children reach maturity without ever having established a mentor/mentee relationship with an adult. Those children will almost inevitably experience a sense of anonymity, and, as discussed earlier, anonymity breeds behavior problems. In fact, many kids with discipline problems act out simply to establish an informal mentorship with an adult—the principal who has to discipline them. Schooling efforts would be so much more effective if a systematic set of procedures was in place whereby mentors are provided for each child at risk for behavior problems.

> One certainty in education is that the needs of each child for attention will be met—no qualifications, no exceptions.

The bottom of Figure 1.1 shows the comprehensive accumulation of the various needs (attention tanks) of the child. As described previously, these needs vary considerably from one child to the next, as well as across the age span. One certainty in education is that the needs of each child for attantion will be met—no qualifications, no exceptions. During the early years of life, the child needs attention to basic survival needs (e.g., food, shelter, companionship), and these are typically met by the family and/or caregivers. During the peer influence period, the survival needs continue, but the child also experiences needs for social attention from his or her peers. Finally, during the last period, the need for self-respect or self-worth is prominent, even though the other needs continue. Given these changing needs, and the differences between individual children, schools must find ways to meet the attention needs of every student in a manner that rewards the student for the behavior teachers want to increase.

Thus, meeting the attention and relationship needs of the child in these phases becomes the focal point for discipline. Given the large number of influences on a child's behavior during any phase, these needs should be viewed as a bubbling caldron of desire for attention from a variety of people. A child's needs are comprised of a set of variables so complex that no behavioral scientist has yet been able to determine accurate maps of these influences. Rather than exact responses to discrete situations, relational discipline is based on formulation of relationships based on the broad understandings represented by this model.

Working within this model, then, are certain general tenets about how behavioral influences impact behavior. For example, operative in this model are rules about who determines what the needs of the child are as well as how attention needs will be met. These are summarized here:

### Tenets of Relational Discipline

1. The most profound disciplinary influences at all points in life are the relationships a person has. Thus, relationships, not specific techniques, are the basis for effective discipline. Schools must attend increasingly to relationships with teachers (i.e., smaller caseloads), relationships between students (i.e., using peer-group influences), use of mentors, and ultimately the development of self-discipline.

2. Kids are attention tanks. Every attention tank will be filled in some manner, either positively or negatively, and kids alone determine how their tanks will be filled.

3. Discipline must progress through predictable developmental levels. Use of the disciplinary influences active on and within each individual at each developmental level will enhance disciplinary effectiveness. Adult-imposed disciplinary strategies must yield to peer-imposed disciplinary tactics, and eventually mature into self-imposed discipline in order for kids to adjust to adult life appropriately.

With the diagram shown in Figure 1.1 and these general tenets, we are now ready to proceed to the specific tactics based on the relational discipline model. Note that other tactics not included here may well work—if the conditions, structure, and rules for relational discipline have been attended to. Also note that many behavioral techniques work, as well, specifically because they address the components of this model.

## References

Bender, W. N. (1999, April 23). *Invisible kids.* A keynote speech delivered to the Doylestown School District, Doylestown, PA.

Bender, W. N., & McLaughlin, P. J. (1997). Weapons violence in schools: Strategies for teachers confronting violence and hostage situations. *Intervention in School and Clinic, 32* (4), 211–216.

Clinton, G., & Miles, W. (1999). Mentoring programs: Fostering resilience in at-risk kids. In W. N. Bender, G. Clinton, & R. L. Bender (Eds.), *Violence prevention and reduction in schools* (pp. 31–46). Austin, TX: Pro-Ed.

Gottfredson, D. (1998). School based crime prevention. In L. W. Sherman, D. Gottfredson, D. MacKenzie, J. Eck, P. Reuter, & S. Bushway (Eds.), *Preventing crime: What works, what doesn't, what's promising.* A report to the United States Congress. Washington, DC: National Institute of Justice.

McPartland, J., Jordan, W., Legters, N., & Balfanz, R. (1997). Finding safety in small numbers. *Educational Leadership, 55* (2), 14–17.

Resnick, M. D., Bearman, P. S., Blum, R. W., Bauman, K. E., Harris, K. M., Jones, J., Tabor, J., Beuhring, T., Sieving, R. E., Shew, M., Ireland, M., Bearinger, L. H., & Udry, R. (1997). Protecting adolescents from harm: Findings from the national longitudinal study on adolescent health. *Journal of the American Medical Association, 278* (10), 823–832.

Sautter, C. (1995). *Standing up to violence.* Bloomington, IN: Kappan Special Report.

Shen, J. (1997). The evolution of violence in schools. *Educational Leadership, 55* (2), 18–21.

Shubert, T. H., Bressette, S., Deeken, J., & Bender, W. N. (1999). Analysis of random school shootings. In W. N. Bender, G. Clinton, & R. L. Bender (Eds.), *Violence prevention and reduction in schools* (pp. 97–102). Austin, TX: Pro-Ed.

Stevens, R. L. (1995). *Violence in the schools.* A presentation on W. N. Bender & R. L. Bender's *Violence in the schools,* a workshop produced by The Teacher's Workshop, Bishop, GA.

Walker, R. (1998, January 13). *Discipline without disruption.* A presentation appearing on W. N. Bender & P. J. McLaughlin's *The tough kid workshop series* of the Interactive Teaching Network, University of Georgia, Athens.

## Chapter 2

# The Aggressive, Noncompliant, or Defiant Kid

Some in-your-face kids are angry. They can be counted on to be defiant, non-compliant, or aggressive—either verbally or physically; they may be hostile toward the teacher and/or other students, or "just plain mean." When these kids appear in class on the first day of the year, an experienced teacher will often have them identified within two hours—certainly within two days. They are that obvious in the classroom, and it seems that every public school class today has one or two such students—some have many more.

> These kids demonstrate a consistent tendency to disrupt the class through aggression, defiance, and/or attention-grabbing behavior.

These students may be identified as having different types of problems—attention deficit hyperactivity disorders (ADHD), oppositional defiant disorders, conduct problems, severe emotional disturbance, or social maladjustment. Regardless of which label is fashionable during any particular year, these kids demonstrate a consistent tendency to disrupt the class through aggression, defiance, and/or attention-grabbing behavior. These are the students who most often play power games with teachers; they can disrupt the class anytime they wish, and this, in their minds, empowers them. They slam books down on the desk, they cuss, they call others names, they have words with other students as they walk by, they bully others, and much more. From the perspective of the teacher, only one thing is certain: With these students in the class, there will be behavior problems.

Walker and Sylwester (1998) identified four types of noncompliance that teachers find highly disruptive:

1. *Passive noncompliance:* The child hears the instruction to do something but resists performing the task.
2. *Simple refusal:* The child acknowledges the request but verbally refuses to do the task.
3. *Direct defiance:* The child responds to a task directive by anger, hostility, and direct defiance (e.g., insulting the teacher and/or name-calling).
4. *Negotiation:* The child attempts to bargain with the teacher.

As you may well imagine, any of these responses to a teacher's directive can be quite disruptive in the typical classroom, and teachers seem to be increasingly confronted with these forms of noncompliance.

Upon reflection, most teachers agree that the students who demonstrate this array of behavioral problems seem to know and understand when and why they disrupt the class. In fact, many teachers begin to sense that disruptions occur in some "strategic" moment—perhaps just prior to a change of subjects or immediately after a seatwork assignment has been made. In that way, the inappropriate behavior may influence the work expectations of the student or of the class. For example, when a seatwork assignment is made, the so-called problem student slams his or her book shut and says to the teacher, "You go to hell! I'm not going to do it!"

When confronted with this overt and disruptive defiance, the teacher may be lured in and engaged in a power play created by the student; the teacher may even respond with mild punishments or by sending the student to the office. In turn, this gives the student the excuse needed to ignore the teacher and avoid doing the work. Thus, the behavior has resulted in what the student may have desired in the first place—work avoidance—making this a strategic behavior on the part of the child.

> No teacher can *make* a child do anything.

Of course, it is a fact of life in the classroom that no teacher can *make* a child do anything. Teachers can reinforce and punish children (within limits), structure interesting activities, or even fail the student for the year, but forcing a child to do a single assignment, once a child has decided not to do it, is not possible. Thus, this type of power play—this strategically defiant behavior—can be a difficult problem for many teachers. Because students are quite likely to invest more energy in the power play than the teacher can, the teacher simply cannot win in most power-play situations.

Note, too, that this type of behavior seems to be developmental, to some degree; it is much more frequent as students get beyond the lower elementary grades. Interestingly, most students identified for special services have traditionally been identified around the third or fourth grade, and this age range immediately precedes the years during which the peer group assumes more influence in behavior. Thus, for students who are consistently aggressive, defiant, and/or attention seeking in a strategic sense, tactics that focus on both their self-image (i.e., their perceived personal power) and on use of the influence of the peer group are particularly appropriate.

> To be effective in discipline, teachers must establish a personal relationship with these students.

In order to be effective in discipline, teachers must establish a personal relationship with these students, even though these kids are some of the most difficult with whom to work. Regardless of how experienced teachers are, they may find themselves actively disliking these students; thus, the relational discipline concept would suggest that little discipline will be possible. Clearly, the teacher must find a way both to allow this student some personal power, and thereby demonstrate respect for the student, and to encourage respect from the student for the teacher's role and for others in the classroom. In short, effective teachers learn to avoid power plays with students.

## Defusing the Time Bomb: Avoiding Power Plays

Preventing the escalation of a power play is a critical skill for teachers who wish to establish a positive relationship with troubled students. Numerous authors have indicated that the most effective thing a teacher can do is to choose not to play the game (Albert, 1996; Walker & Sylwester, 1998). Walker (1998) indicated that in 75 percent of the cases in which teachers are physically attacked, there is some "prelude" that involves an escalating power play with a student. Thus, avoiding power plays with students is not only effective from a disciplinary standpoint but it is also the safe choice for teachers from a physical standpoint.

In avoiding power plays, several cautions should always be kept in mind (Albert, 1996; Walker, 1998). First, when a teacher, parent, or parapro-

*"But, Miss Jones, I don't see anything about*
*strangulation in Billy's behavior management plan."*

fessional engages in a power struggle with a student, the student will always win. In simple terms, the student can always invest himself or herself totally in the power struggle, whereas the teacher cannot. Thus, teachers are at a disadvantage in any building power play. The adult might eventually be able to elicit compliance, but the student has controlled the situation.

Second, teachers should always avoid power plays; in other words, they should never accept the student's challenge (i.e., the shouted defiance or the inappropriate behavior offered as a challenge to authority). Rather, teachers should have a series of options available (discussed next) for use when a student begins a power play. Effective options for the teacher to use in defusing the ticking time bomb of aggression will greatly enhance the relationship between the teacher and the student over the long term.

Third, teachers should structure interactions with students based on the development of mutual respect. They must take the initiative and find ways to single out the most difficult students for something positive, realizing that the task of building rapport with many in-your-face kids will take a considerable amount of time. Teachers' persistence in that effort is *critical*—if the first three attempts to defuse a power play don't work, try something else.

## The Techniques

Teachers should be prepared, on a moment's notice, to use a variety of defusing techniques to escape from the building power struggle. These various techniques, which come from a variety of sources (Albert, 1996; Colvin, Ainge, & Nelson, 1997; Walker & Sylwester, 1998; Walker, 1998), generally allow the teacher to escape power plays with students.

### Repeat the Instructions

If a student shouts angrily that he or she won't do an assignment, merely repeat the instructions in a calm voice two or three times each time the student challenges you. Use a quieter voice each time, and call the student's name. Calling a student's name quietly can have a very calming effect in many situations. After three or four repetitions of the instructions, you should merely turn, walk away, and begin to assist another student. Let the offending student calm down. If an explosion occurs, you will need to use another harsher disciplinary technique.

### Use Humor

On occasion, humor can defuse a student's anger, as long as the humor is not directed at the student (Albert, 1996). You could perhaps try to joke about the noncompliance. Statements such as, "Well, that's one way to go," may allow you to escape an overt power play and continue the lesson. In this instance, no joke should be made about the particular defiant student. Clearly, this recommendation to use humor should not be interpreted as an opportunity to do so at the students' expense. Also, never use humiliation as a disciplinary tool. Such negative use of humor detracts from the efforts to build positive relationships with students.

### Inquire about a Student's Anger

On some occasions, you might wish to inquire about the student's anger, such as, "I can see that the assignment upsets you. Is it something we can talk calmly about?" The wise teacher would rather have a brief discussion about the student's concern, and then return to the assignment, than have an escalating power struggle. Be cautious with this technique, however, since you may find yourself "trapped" in a lengthy discussion. In fact, if students learn that teachers are willing to talk about problems, some students will intentionally use this strategy to avoid assignments.

### Share Power

If a student challenges you on an assignment or task, and mentions something else he or she would like to do, be prepared to negotiate and share power concerning when the tasks may be done (Colvin, Ainge, & Nelson, 1997). Even a small acknowledgment of the student's power can often avoid a major explosion for many kids.

### Postpone the Discussion

Finally, postponing a discussion may be an appropriate tactic (Albert, 1996). If a student is highly emotionally charged (i.e., very angry or upset), let the student know that you want to discuss that with him or her, but that the discussion may be held only at the end of the period, when your time is free. Sometimes, merely knowing that a caring adult in the setting is interested can defuse a building problem.

Clearly, teachers who wish to establish a positive relationship with students should not engage in power plays created by the student, but rather find ways to avoid the initial power play and then positively influence these students toward more appropriate behaviors. Thus, after the initial explosion (or the potential for the initial explosion) is dealt with, teachers will need one or more tactics that will alleviate the problem. The section below presents two very effective, yet highly different, methods for fostering respect for in-your-face kids, respect for the classroom community, and respect for all members of the community: peer confrontation and responsibility strategies.

## *Removing the Audience:*
## *The Peer Confrontation Technique*

> The focus on development of relationships is paramount, and the relationships that students have with their peers are a crucial influence on behavior after grade 4 or 5.

Peer confrontation is an in-your-face type of disciplinary strategy that is appropriate for many elementary, middle, junior high, and high school students. In relational discipline, the focus on development of relationships is paramount, and the relationships that students have with their peers are a crucial influence on behavior after grade 4 or 5. Various researchers have long advocated using peer groups to assist in facilitating positive behavior or to elicit openness among students (Salend, Whittaker, & Reeder, 1992; Sandler, Arnold, Gable, & Strain, 1987; Tanaka & Reid, 1997). With the major emphasis on relationships, a focus on positive use of peer relationships seems a natural application of relational discipline.

This tactic is appropriate slightly before, during, and after the peer influence period, and is totally dependent on the use of the peers in the class. As students reach the middle grades, peers become increasingly important as a referent for behavior, whereas parents, teachers, and other adults provide this referent during the earlier years. This is not to suggest that parents and teachers become unimportant in disciplining young adolescents. In fact, early adolescence may ultimately be shown to be a crucial time for parents and teachers to exert positive influences. Still, the peers become an increasingly important disciplinary influence during these middle elementary school years, and teachers must take advantage of that fact.

Perception, during these years, is the key to behavior. The identity of adolescents is heavily tied to what they believe others perceive about them. In fact, kids at this age often feel as if their entire lives are something of a play or performance that they put on for their peers. This is the time at which personal appearance becomes increasingly important, and one component of personal appearance is a student's desire to look quite different from his or her parents. Early adolescents begin to dress and act much more like each other, and this should yield insight on who truly influences children's behavior.

Perception is the key to behavior. The identity of adolescents is heavily tied to what they believe others perceive about them.

In addition to this growing concern with the perception of others, the attention tank needs of the child are still present. This leads to a natural transition in which young adolescents (ages 11 to 14) begin to "show off" increasingly for their peers. Youngsters will begin to entertain their peers through bizarre or inappropriate behaviors, even at the expense of being ridiculed as the class clown. Others may begin seriously bullying their peers, since this, like the need to entertain, results in getting their attention needs met.

The peer confrontation strategy, then, is useful during this phase of disciplinary development because it addresses the attention tank needs of the child, as well as the growing role of the peers in influencing behavior. Thus, the peer confrontation strategy is used for three reasons: (1) to remove the audience for inappropriate behaviors, (2) to elicit the appropriate behavior through the use of peer pressure, and (3) to help students develop an understanding of their own behavior. Each of these three effects may be easily accomplished if the tactic is applied appropriately in the correct situation.

## When to Try Peer Confrontation

If you wish to get rid of the "audience" for misbehavior and get that audience working *for* you rather than *against* you, the peer confrontation strategy is the tactic for you.

Almost every middle school teacher has seen kids who show off through misbehavior—including defiant and aggressive behavior—for the other students in their class. Young adolescents who misbehave are often rewarded by peer-group admiration, and this can lead to increased behavior problems. If you have students who are using their defiance as a means to earn attention from their peers or to play off the attention of other students in your class, or if you wish to get rid of the "audience" for misbehavior and get that audience working *for* you rather than *against* you, the peer confrontation strategy is the tactic for you. Because peers begin to have influence in the early middle school years, this strategy is appropriate in grade levels as low as fourth grade up through the high school years.

Unlike some of the other tactics covered in this book, the peer confrontation strategy is useful for situations in which students are angry or heavily emotionally involved in other ways. Even when students have come to blows, or are about to, after the students are separated and the overt violence has stopped, a peer confrontation strategy can be applied. Thus, for kids who consistently bully others, who overtly act out, who are attention seeking, or who use fists to get attention or to get their own way, this strategy is useful.

For the lone bully in the class, peer confrontation is particularly appropriate. Most bullys are demonstrating power behavior that they have learned at home, and some may not realize how class members really feel about their behavior. Others may use their bullying behavior to elicit attention—again, a strategic behavior that accomplishes a goal for the bully.

> Embarrassment is not intended as the primary result of this strategy, and if a child is particularly easy to embarrass, this is probably not an appropriate strategy.

There are some students for whom this strategy is not appropriate. Of course, the strategy should be avoided if less intrusive strategies work, but it

*Billy, it's not good manners to break your pencil, desk, and classmate.*

should likewise be avoided if a particular child seems devastated by even the smallest degree of class attention or embarrassment. Many teachers have had the experience of teaching intensely shy students or students who would feel particularly sensitive to any open discussion of their behavior. Although some embarrassment will be the natural by-product of this strategy, the strategy is intended primarily to remove the audience that supports misbehavior (through peer attention, etc.) and to help kids analyze their behavior and find ways to get their needs met without misbehavior. Embarrassment is not intended as the primary result of this strategy, and if a child is particularly easy to embarrass, this is probably not an appropriate strategy.

Another consideration: This strategy is dependent on some mild social pressure from peers; therefore, it might not be effective in situations in which a student is primarily socialized to students other than those in the class. Some students may respond only to peer pressure from certain peers; for example, this may happen with some gang members, since these students are usually socialized to care only about the opinions of other gang members. In that case, this procedure can exert very little social pressure, since those students typically are so involved in the gang that only peer pressure from other gang members will be effective. In those situations, another tactic should be used.

### Implementing Peer Confrontation

When a student consistently interrupts the class or demonstrates a problematic behavior, the teacher should take some type of baseline data on how often that occurs. A simple frequency count will usually suffice for this. For example, imagine that you teach in a sixth-grade classroom in which Billy Bender enjoys widespread audience attention for cursing in class. Needless to say, each time Billy cusses in class, the class snickers until you can reestablish control. Four weeks ago, as a result of Billy's cursing, you sent him to the principal, and the next week you called his parents in for a conference, with little results.

You have decided to take a more proactive step, and use a peer confrontation approach. Figure 2.1 presents a frequency count of how many times Billy cursed in class. Information for this chart was collected for three weeks during the morning instructional period (i.e., the period between the first bell and recess). To collect this information, you merely had to mark on your notepad each time Billy cursed. In short, this type of data can be collected without disturbing the instruction in the class.

The peer confrontation technique is appropriate when a student dem-

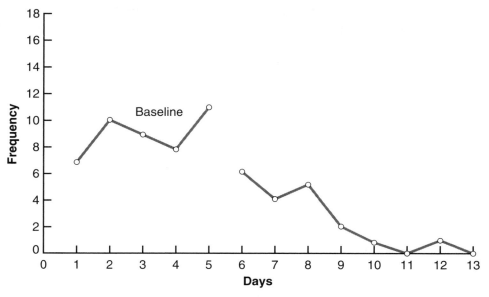

The data in the baseline period indicate that Billy was cussing, on average, nine times during the five-day baseline phase. However, after the implementation of the peer confrontation procedure, note that Billy's cussing decreased to less than one outburst per day for the last several days. Using peer confrontation provides a powerful tool for the teacher to decrease unwanted behavior.

**FIGURE 2.1**   *Intervention Data on Cussing in Class*

onstrates the misbehavior a number of times during a single day (say 8 to 25 misbehaviors). As this example demonstrates, a simple count of the frequency of the misbehavior during a particular class over a three-day, or perhaps a five-day, period will provide enough data to demonstrate a very disruptive problem behavior.

## Step 1: Begin the Intervention

When Billy demonstrates the misbehavior for the first time after the baseline data are completed, you begin the technique through the use of questions that are intended both to defuse the situation and to elicit the assistance of the class in analysis of it. The following sample dialogue provides examples of what you might say when Billy demonstrates a problem behavior, and the types of responses that other students in the class may give. In a voice loud enough to get every student's attention, you begin the strategy:

"Wait a minute, everyone. We just saw an inappropriate behavior that disrupted our work. What problem behavior did we all just see?"

The focus should be on the misbehavior and not who did it. Other statements to use may include:

"We're going to stop class right now because something important just happened that messed up our worktime. Can anyone describe the behavior problem that just happened, please? Raise your hand if you can."

The desired response is to have another student in the class accurately describe the behavior problem that disrupted the class, without mentioning or criticizing the offending student. Thus, the statements you make should focus not only on the behavior problem but on the disruption (i.e., the "offense") to the class. Of course, the students will not realize what this new procedure is the first time it is attempted. Students may accurately identify the behavior, but you might also get a response such as the following:

"Billy is being a jerk."

Clearly, this is not where you want the discussion to go. So, you stop this dialogue by a mild punishment to the student who called Billy a name. You might step toward the student who did the name-calling (a somewhat aggressive and thus punishing move), and say:

"No! We do not call other students names in this class. I want to know what behavior just occurred that stopped us from doing our work."

After this statement, you step back and disengage from the student who did the name-calling. At some point, you will get a student to give you a one-sentence description of the behavior problem that was observed rather than the name or a criticism of the offending student. For example, some student might say:

"Somebody just cussed in class."

When another class member called Billy a name, you defended Billy!

Prior to moving on with the procedure, let's analyze the process up to this point. Thus far, Billy has disrupted class and yet you haven't even looked in his direction. In fact, when another class memeber called Billy a name, you defended Billy! At this point, Billy is in shock, because he expected some punishment but he hasn't received it; in fact, you defended him, and that alone will empower you in this situation. Further, you have effectively removed Billy's audience. The class is looking at you now rather than snickering at Billy. Each of these results is a positive result of this procedure.

### Step 2: Analyze the Behavior

At some point, a student will give you a response that focuses on the behavior without mentioning Billy's name. When this happens, you elicit interaction to analyze the behavior. The following questions can work for this:

**"Can anyone guess why someone might do that?"**
**"Why would anyone do that?"**

> Billy is now listening to his peers very cooly and critically analyze his behavior.

You want the class to participate with you in stating possible reasons for the misbehavior. Still somewhat puzzled, Billy is now listening to his peers very coolly and critically analyze his behavior. Again, this is a powerful deterrent and further empowers you. The first set of reasons mentioned by other students for the misbehavior can lead into a positive discussion of behavioral options. Students may suggest that a kid curses because he wants attention or can't do the work. You should elicit several responses from other students about why this misbehavior might occur, and compliment each student who provides a reasonable response. You now have the class critically analyzing a misbehavior rather than snickering and serving as an audience for Billy's inappropriate behavior. Note, also, that you still haven't engaged with Billy to this point.

### Step 3: Create Other Options

Next, you want the class to continue their problem solving by suggesting other options for when a kid wants attention or cannot do the work. You can elicit these options by the following types of statements:

**"Can we suggest other things someone might do if he needs help?"**
**"We are not here to criticize anyone, but we do want to help everyone control their temper and stop cussing. Can someone suggest what a student may want to do when he feels he is getting angry?"**

Ideally, responses from the class will involve more constructive options to frustration. Possible answers from the class may include:

**"Put his head down."**
**"Raise his hand and ask for help."**

> In a situation where Billy thought he would get a great deal of positive attention from his peers, he has instead had his behavior coolly and critically analyzed by them.

Again, let's analyze what has happened in the class to this point. First of all, Billy has heard you defend him when other class members called him a name. This alone can have powerful effects with some kids. Next, in a situation where Billy thought he would get a great deal of positive attention from his peers, he has instead had his behavior coolly and critically analyzed by them. This is very punishing for most preadolescents and adolescents. Also, so far, you have not even looked in his direction. Finally, note that even if this procedure is a flop as an intervention for Billy, the rest of the class has engaged in a two- to three-minute problem-solving discussion about appropriate and inappropriate behavioral options. What classroom in any public school today would not benefit from such a discussion? Further, the positive effects of this procedure on other class members shouldn't be overlooked. Other students may begin to respond more appropriately in class, even when this procedure is used for someone else.

### Step 4: Elicit Student Participation

This step represents a critical decision on your part. Your goal is to discuss the problem behavior and the behavioral options with Billy and to get him to "buy into" trying the solution(s) that the class offered. This may be accomplished by turning to Billy immediately after the class has completed the two- to three-minute problem-solving discussion and requesting that he try these ideas. However, for some behaviors (e.g., fighting and overt name-calling), disruptive students might be too emotionally charged after this procedure to choose to participate in it at that point. Thus, you must make a choice about when to invite Billy's participation in the solutions offered. If Billy seems calm, then you should continue the procedure in class by moving into this step. Alternatively, if Billy is still highly charged, angry, or appears frustrated, you should wait until the end of class and pull Billy aside for this final step. Typically, for most problem behaviors, a later individual conversation with the student will work best, since students will often be angry at having "their" audience removed.

However, the decision on when to hold this brief conference with the student is solely up to you. If, in your view, Billy is not overly excited after the class has analyzed and discussed his behavior, you might elicit his participation by turning to him in class and saying:

**"Billy, would you like to try doing that with the help of the class? We'd all like to help you stop cussing so we can continue our work."**

Again, note the last phrase of this statement—a phrase that emphasizes the need of the class not to be disrupted. At this point, if Billy indicates a willingness to try the options offered, you merely indicate to the class that the problem has been dealt with and that the other class members should resume their work. Alternatively, if Billy is too emotionally charged to participate in this step at that time, you simply turn to the class after step 3 (see above), without even engaging Billy, and instruct them to begin their work. Billy, likewise should be instructed to get back to work. In this case, after class you should again try to get Billy to consider the options that the class generated.

## Advantages of the Peer Confrontation Procedure

There are a number of advantages of this procedure that make it a powerful option for the teacher:

1. This procedure is a disciplinary option for in-your-face kids that you can use for overt behavior problems (cussing, lying, bullying, fighting, etc.) while avoiding a direct power struggle. It allows you to effectively discipline proactively, using the power of the peer group without engaging in a power struggle with a misbehaving student.

2. This is a powerful procedure in that the audience for misbehavior is decisively removed from the student. You can get the class working on your side to promote positive behavior.

3. Even if this procedure fails for a particular student, you have still engaged with the class in a problem-solving approach to behavior problems, and the students have seen you respond in a nonaggressive fashion to a misbehavior that angered you. Thus, the class has not only benefited from witnessing a problem-solving approach to a disruption but they have also witnessed a mature, nonaggressive approach to that disruption. From your classroom model on this approach, many students will learn this approach to problem solving.

4. The "learning curve" of the class will increase over time. In other words, once the procedure has been used for one student, the class can more easily help you apply it for other kids, too! Further, the class will quickly learn that you will not tolerate name-calling in this disciplinary procedure, but rather that you will praise kids who focus on discussion of problem behaviors.

5. Time is another advantage. The first time you do this procedure with the class, it will take approximately four or five minutes, but after several occurrences, you will see the time drop to two to three minutes. Almost any classroom can profit from the brief periodic discussions of appropriate behavior that this procedure facilitates.

6. Perhaps the most important advantage of this strategy is that it offers you an optional response to misbehavior that not only avoids a power

play but also holds open the opportunity for establishing a helping relationship with a student. When the strategy is done well, you will be perceived as assisting the student develop a method to control his temper (or cursing, etc.). Thus, as emphasized by the concept of relational discipline, you have not compromised your relationship with the student by using this strategy. In fact, when kids get angry as a result of this strategy, they are more often angry at other class members than at the teacher, for the teacher is seen as a helper.

### Using Peer Confrontation

This peer confrontation procedure offers you an option to use with almost any overly disruptive student, and this is particularly appropriate for the defiant student. From the relational discipline perspective, the strategy empowers you, the teacher, by obtaining the cooperation of the peer group in confronting a student about his or her unacceptable behavior. The procedure focuses on the relationship between the misbehaving student and his or her peers, and uses the power of those relationships to foster appropriate behavior. Because of the use of the peer group, this strategy can be a powerful deterrent for misbehavior of almost any sort during the peer influence period.

Box 2.1 presents, in a nutshell, the guidelines for the peer confrontation procedure. You might want to duplicate this information for parents, students, and other educators when explaining the procedure to them.

## Making a Difference: The Responsibility Strategy

Responsibility strategies focus on gaining positive attention for a student by assisting the student in identifying his or her responsibilities to teachers, classmates, and the school. As the attention tank concept suggests, defiant, acting-out students are often motivated by a desire for attention—whether it be positive or negative. These students derive a certain amount of personal power from oppositional or defiant misbehavior. During the misbehavior, the attention of the class is centered on them, and the teacher must attend in some fashion to the misbehavior; this is a powerful position for a student to be in. Oppositional students often find that most of their recognition comes from situations in which they misbehave.

One effective strategy to use with these kids is based on finding creative ways for offering attention to students who need to demonstrate their personal power in order to fill their attention tanks. Using these students for individual responsibilities allows them the opportunity to "show off" in an

## BOX 2.1 • *Peer Confrontation Strategy Guidelines*

### When Should I Try It?

Peer confrontation is an appropriate strategy for many middle, junior high, and high school students. As students reach the middle grades, peers become increasingly important as a referent for behavior. For this reason, students who misbehave are often rewarded by peer-group admiration, and this leads to behavior problems. If you have students who are playing off the attention of others, and you wish to get the audience for misbehavior working for you rather than against you, try this idea! The peer confrontation strategy is used for three reasons:

1. To remove the audience for inappropriate behaviors
2. To elicit the appropriate behavior through the use of mild peer pressure
3. To help students develop an understanding of their own behavior

### What Do I Do First?

When a student consistently disrupts class, take some type of baseline data. This technique is appropriate when a student demonstrates the misbehavior a number of times during a single day (say 8 to 15 misbehaviors). A simple count of the frequency of the misbehavior during a particular class will provide enough data to demonstrate the problem behavior.

### The Intervention

On the day after baseline, when the student demonstrates the misbehavior, you begin the technique through the use of questions that are intended both to defuse the situation and to elicit the assistance of the class in analysis of it. In a voice loud enough to get everyone's attention, you should say:

**"Wait a minute, everyone. We just saw an inappropriate behavior that disrupted class. What problem behavior did we all just see?"**

The focus should be on the misbehavior and the resulting disruption, not on who did it. Other statements to use include:

**"We're going to stop class right now because something important just happened that disturbed class. Can anyone describe the behavior problem that just happened, please? Raise your hand if you can."**

The desired response is to have the students describe the behavior accurately without naming or criticizing the offending student. If the first remark is overtly critical, you should respond with a caution about criticism and a desire to assist the student who just demonstrated the behavior problem. Then focus on why a student might misbehave in that way:

**"Can anyone guess why someone might do that misbehavior?"**

*(continued)*

## BOX 2.1   Continued

You want the class to participate with you in stating possible reasons for the misbehavior (e.g., attention seeking, can't do the work so he or she misbehaves, etc.). You now have the class critically analyzing a misbehavior rather than snickering at the disruptive student.

**"Can we suggest other behaviors?"**

Next, you want the class to generate behavioral options with you, such as "Put his head down," "Turn away," or "Walk back to his seat."

At this point, you address the offending student and ask:

**"Would you like to try doing that instead of (whatever the problem behavior is) with the help of the class?"**

Your goal is to try to elicit the student's cooperation.

*Suggestions to Make This Work in Your Class*

1. In some cases, it may be necessary to talk with the student after class (after he or she has calmed down a bit), show him or her the baseline data, and encourage willing participation.
2. Share the project with the principal and the parents as soon as the student chooses to cooperate.
3. If the student becomes highly uncomfortable and indicates that he or she feels the project is an effort for the class to "gang up on me," discontinue the project and select another procedure. The intent is to get the student to think objectively about his or her behavior, not to overtly embarrass him or her.
4. Use this strategy with students with overt conduct problems, including aggression, as long as the students ares not explosive.
5. Try this strategy first with a student in the class who is not your biggest behavior problem. In this fashion, the class learns how to participate in the technique before you apply it to the student you wish to use it for.

appropriate way; further, the tasks done by these students may even assist the teacher or others in the class.

> If students who are aggressive, defiant, and oppositional can find ways to demonstrate their personal authority and power in productive ways, they will not need to demonstrate their power in disruptive ways.

In formulating the concept of relational discipline, I have used the term *responsibility strategies* to highlight the critical factor in this tactic—the need to give kids some meaningful responsibility that they wish to take and that allows them to receive attention for possible demonstrations of their personal power. Such demonstrations not only fill the attention tank needs of the students but they also modify the students' relationships with the teacher and/or others in the classroom, putting those relationships on a more positive basis. If students who are aggressive, defiant, and oppositional can find ways to demonstrate their personal authority and power in productive ways, they will not need to demonstrate their power in disruptive ways. Several examples will help to illustrate this strategy.

Dr. Bob Brooks, former principal of a lock-door school unit in a psychiatric hospital for difficult kids, often tells of a kid who broke every lightbulb he could get to within the school. All lights were fair game, and he really didn't care what disciplinary measures were used to punish him for breaking lightbulbs—he was going to break them anyway. This was, quite blatantly, an oppositional and attention-getting misbehavior on the part of the student.

To Dr. Brooks's credit, he reflected on that student's relationship to the class and the school in general and then he took a chance: Dr. Brooks made that student the "Lightbulb Monitor" for the school. Each day, the kid was encouraged to roam the halls for a brief period, visit each room, and assure that each and every lightbulb was working properly. When lightbulbs were out, the student had the responsibility of reporting the problem to the office. Of course, the kid loved going into a room of his peers each morning—filled with his own importance—and switching on the lights several times while the teacher checked attendance. His peers saw that he was given special privileges, along with his special responsibility, and that attention from his peers made a positive difference in this student's behavior. This responsibility strategy ended the lightbulb breaking by this student, but perhaps the more important point is that this kid had a responsibility—a meaningful contribution to make to the school—for perhaps the first time in his school career.

A more poignant example of a responsibility strategy comes from Dr. Charles Maher (1982, 1984) of Rutgers University. Dr. Maher reported several research studies in which adolescents with horrible behavior records were used as tutors for students with mental disabilities in lower grade levels. Now, upon initial reflection, this tactic seems frightening for any experienced educator. Imagine finding the "last-chance" students—that is, adolescent males and females who had been identified during the middle and junior high years as socially maladjusted and emotionally disturbed because of violence, aggression, and/or other severe behavioral problems—and using them as tutors! In a very real sense, this took courage.

There was the potential that these adolescents in middle and junior high would actually victimize the students from grades 2 and 3 whom they were tutoring.

Instead, the opposite occurred. In the controlled study, the behavior of the socially maladjusted, conduct-problem students used as tutors improved *drastically*, compared to another group of similar students who merely received peer counseling. The number of disciplinary problems for the tutors went down, their attendance improved, and their tutoring even assisted them academically.

Further, anecdotal observations suggest that the *responsibility* of tutoring seemed to be the deciding factor. By virtue of tutoring, these kids were seen as "leaders" in some sense. Specifically, the behavior-problem adolescents began to "own" their tutees, "protecting" them on the playground and playing and interacting with them. In the face of these surprising findings, Dr. Maher repeated this experimental study in 1984, just to assure that the first results were valid. The results of the second project were the same. Tutoring gave these behavior-problem kids a responsibility for others—a meaningful connection to others in the school—and it drastically improved their behavior. More recently, these positive behavioral results have also been demonstrated in other studies that used students with behavior problems as tutors (Lazerson, Foster, Brown, & Hummel, 1988).

> The adolescents were invited to *contribute* something—they were given a responsibility that they thought important.

Of course, with limited academic skills themselves, the tutors would not have been appropriate for use as tutors of same-age peers. However, using these kids who had serious behavior problems as tutors of younger children with mild intellectual disabilities on simple reading tasks worked wonderfully. Again, the adolescents were invited to *contribute* something— they were given a responsibility that they though important.

### With Whom Should This Strategy Be Used?

One key indicator on when to use this strategy is the frequency of the behavior problem. When teachers or administrators have a student who demonstrates disciplinary problems very frequently, it seems as though the same type of problem was dealt with yesterday—or perhaps only 15 minutes ago—from the same student. Students who are constantly in the principal's office for misbehavior are good candidates for the use of the responsibility strategy. These students are typically unconnected with the school environment and/or others within that environment. Some specific set of responsibilities, individually selected for the student, may result in reconnecting the student emotionally to the school, establishing a basis for positive relationships and improving behavior.

The responsibility strategies fit the need in a number of situations in which students are angry, aggressive, or oppositional. After the immediate behavioral concern is over, the teacher talks with the student about how the student can "assist" in the class, using his or her leadership skills. Thus, this is a useful strategy for kids who consistently act out or who use violence to get attention.

Unlike the peer confrontation strategy discussed earlier, the responsibility strategy is often effective with gang members and other students who are primarily socialized to small gang-like groups in the class or school. There are examples in which gang members have taken on the responsibility of policing the playground or hallways and maintaining peace (under the supervision of teachers, of course). If responsibilities can be identified that allow gang members to demonstrate their power in positive ways (without putting other students at risk—a critical concern!), this can be a very effective strategy, since it recognizes the power of the student in a way in which the teacher finds it acceptable.

There are some kids for whom this strategy is not appropriate. For students with explosive tendencies—students who generally behave fairly well but occasionally blow up—other strategies may be more effective (see Chapter 3). Also, one must carefully select a task or responsibility which can be successfully completed by the student in question. The responsibilities should not "challenge" the student (e.g., don't use tutoring academic tasks that tax the tutor academically), but rather allow the student an opportunity to succeed and thus to receive positive attention.

## Implementing Responsibility Strategies

When you see a kid repeatedly in trouble, the immediate violence or disruption can usually be dealt with through a postponement. This is the first step in implementing responsibility strategies.

Walker and Sylwester (1998) suggest disengagement prior to the escalation of a power struggle with the offending student. For example, you may merely inform the student in a relatively soft voice that you and he or she will need to schedule a conference about the misbehavior. You should then turn away from the student and attempt to get the others in class to refocus on the classwork at hand.

Next, reflect on the student's relationship with you and others in the school. It is often effective to mentally take several steps back and ask:

**"How has this student been invited to positively contribute to this school (or this class) today?"**

> A wise educator will try to find ways to involve a student—to make the student feel special—by inviting him or her to contribute in an appropriate way.

This statement is phrased very carefully: Note the use of the term *invited*. Has the student been *invited* to demonstrate his capabilities, her talents, his leadership skills, her opportunities to present a positive self to the school class? In some cases, the answer is probably that the student hasn't been effectively invited to make an appropriate and meaningful contribution. Recall the fundamental rule of the attention tank: A kid will get the attention he or she requires, and if getting the required attention means being defiant, then the kid will most assuredly be defiant. A wise educator will try to find ways to involve a student—to make the student feel special—by inviting him or her to contribute in an appropriate way.

### Why Give a Behavior-Problem Kid Responsibility?

Most of us remember dusting the erasers, cleaning the blackboard for teachers, and doing other "teacher's helper" jobs as privileges in the classrooms of our youth. With a moment's reflection, we can remember how special—how important and involved—those relatively boring and mundane tasks made us feel. Of course, the kids with behavior problems in our classes didn't get to do those jobs because those tasks were usually used as privileges or rewards for good behavior. In fact, in presenting this idea around the country, I have realized that many teachers feel it may be inappropriate to "reward" misbehavior by using these aggressive and defiant kids for special tasks or responsibilities. Indeed, rewarding misbehavior with a serious responsibility does seem to go against all behavioral training (which may be yet another failure of behaviorism—the tendency to reward only the good kids).

Nevertheless, with some kids, offering an attention-generating responsibility will be just the ticket to turn negative behavior into positive behavior, and thereby improve the student's relationship to the teacher and others in the class. Research and anecdotal evidence document the value of this strategy. Also, oppositional, aggressive, and defiant students are typically kids who do not respond to more moderate forms of reward and punishment. In fact, by the time you consider using the responsibility strategies for a student with behavior problems, you have probably already tried everything else—so, at that point, you have nothing to lose by giving the kid a serious responsibility. Why not try something relatively novel?

### What Tasks Seem to Work?

In seeking an appropriate task, consider the interests and desires of the student, his or her capabilities, and the needs of the classroom. The possible task options are almost endless—this is why I sometimes refer to the *responsibility strategies* in the plural. The actual task assigned is relatively unimportant, and almost any necessary task (or even some unnecessary ones, such as lightbulb monitor) will do. Two things are important:

> The student must have impressive "bragging rights" for the opportunity to do the task, and the task must be valued by the student.

1. The student must feel that he or she is truly given an opportunity to contribute. In other words, the student must have impressive "bragging rights" for the opportunity to do the task.
2. The student must believe that the task is important and must be made to feel like a contributing partner in a task that he or she values. The following jobs might help you get started:

> Tutor in a lower-grade class.
> Work as a peer buddy.
> Be a "helper" to another student.
> Empty the trash cans.
> Be a "Clean Room" helper.
> Serve as Playground Monitor.

### Finding the Right Responsibility

How can you find the "right" responsibility for a troublesome student? Often, the student's actions will tell you. For example, the kid described earlier was fixated on lightbulbs, and the role of Lightbulb Monitor was perfectly appropriate for him. Try to consider a student's hobbies and interests as well as the needs of your class or your school. Does your school need pictures taken? Could you use someone to report gang graffiti? Might adjudicated delinquents, supervised by teachers, take some responsibility for notifying teachers about verbal fights on the playground? If planned appropriately, any of these tasks could represent an effective contribution to the school and a positive responsibility for troublesome students.

Of course, in selecting the responsibility, you should consider issues such as the student's confidentiality, privacy, safety, and legal liability. For example, don't appoint a Bathroom Monitor unless you want some kid peeking into stalls. Further, no student's responsibility should require that he or she leave campus or get involved in physical altercations that have already begun between other students. The principal, because of required training in school law and policy, might be the appropriate contact when considering responsibilities that involve students leaving the classroom. Also, supervision should always be available for any student completing his or her responsibility.

In addition to routine supervision, remember that students may need to be more closely supervised the first few times they try out their responsibilities. In implementing tutoring, as described earlier in this chapter, you should consider how and what type of training to offer tutors. How much supervision will be necessary for those tutors, and what types of reinforcement can be offered them? For example, do they get to leave the classroom a few minutes early to go to tutoring? Leaving the classroom takes place in front of the peers and indicates a great deal of trust, thus providing a great deal of reinforcement, even for many kids with serious behavior problems.

Box 2.2 presents step-by-step guidelines for implementing responsibility strategies for giving offending students positive attention.

### Using the Responsibility Strategy

With these concerns in mind, be as creative as necessary but remember: When defiant and aggressive kids can't get the attention they require through positive means, they will always—and I do mean always—get it in some fashion, usually through negative behavior. The use of responsibility strategies, then, can save you a great deal of grief and stress.

## The Challenge of Defiant and Aggressive Kids

For many teachers, defiant, aggressive, or overly violent kids present the biggest single challenge of their careers. These kids are invariably in your face with challenges to the classroom routine and your authority. Having several strategies that seem to work with these kids can make the difference

**BOX 2.2** • *Steps for Implementing Responsibility Strategies*

*Step 1: Deal with Immediate Behavior First*
Use an avoidance or postponement technique, such as:
**"We'll have to discuss this later."**
Resume normal classwork after making your statement.

*Step 2: Consider the Behavior Problems Presented by the Student*
For defiant, aggressive, and oppositional kids, including gang members, responsibility strategies may be your only option.

*Step 3: Reflect on Invitations Offered to the Student*
You should mentally take several steps back and ask:
**"How has this student been invited to positively contribute to this school (or this class) today?"**

*Step 4: Identify Several Potential Responsibilities*
Choose one or two tasks that you think the student will be interested in and agree to do. The task selection should be the kid's interests as well as what is needed in the class or school. Remember that the kid must be made to feel like a contributing partner in a task that he or she values. Examples include:

| | |
|---|---|
| Tutor in a lower-grade class. | Empty the trash cans. |
| Work as a peer buddy. | Be a "Clean Room" helper. |
| Be a "helper" to another student. | Serve as Playground Monitor. |

*Step 5: The Teacher and the Student Jointly Choose a Task*
The student must feel that the task is important, and he or she should be given some choice. Present several choices and be prepared for a discussion with the student to generate others. Select a responsibility task after this discussion and write a one-paragraph description of it and how it is to be done. (This later becomes a signed agreement.)

*Step 6: Discuss the Responsibility with the Student and Principal*
This will highlight the importance of the task for the student as well as inform the principal concerning why the student is doing various tasks around campus. Consider in this meeting the issues of the student's confidentiality, privacy, safety, and legal liability.

*Step 7: Develop a Monitoring Plan for the Task*
This simply written plan should detail the task, when it is to be performed, and how you will monitor the task. The student and you should both sign this agreement.

in the enjoyment that any teacher receives from his or her teaching. For this reason, use of the peer confrontation strategy and the responsibility strategy, when appropriate, offer the option of handling serious behavior problems with relative ease, and still maintaining the ever-critical relationship with these defiant and aggressive students. Your enjoyment of being a teacher will be greatly enhanced if you master these techniques.

## *References*

Albert, L. (1996). *Cooperative discipline*. Circle Pines, MN: American Guidance Service.

Colvin, G., Ainge, D., & Nelson, R. (1997). How to defuse confrontations. *Exceptional Children, 64,* 47–51.

Lazerson, D. B., Foster, H. L., Brown, S. I., & Hummel, J. W. (1988). The effectiveness of cross-age tutoring with truant, junior high school students with learning disabilities. *Journal of Learning Disabilities, 21* (4), 253–255.

Maher, C. A. (1982). Behavioral effects of using conduct problem adolescents as cross-age tutors. *Psychology in the Schools, 19,* 360–364.

Maher, C. A. (1984). Handicapped adolescents as cross-age tutors: Program description and evaluation. *Exceptional Children, 51,* 56–63.

Salend, S. J., Whittaker, C. R., & Reeder, E. (1992). Group evaluation: A collaborative, peer-mediated behavior management system. *Exceptional Children, 59,* 203–209.

Sandler, A. G., Arnold, L. B., Gable, R. A., & Strain, R. A. (1987). Effects of peer pressure on disruptive behavior of behavioral disordered classmates. *Behavioral Disorders, 12,* 104–110.

Tanaka, G., & Reid, K. (1997). Peer helpers: Encouraging kids to confide. *Educational Leadership, 55* (2), 29–32.

Walker, H. M., & Sylwester, R. (1998). Reducing students' refusal and resistance. *Teaching Exceptional Children, 30* (6), 52–58.

Walker, R. (1998, January 19). *Discipline without disruption.* A presentation appearing on W. N. Bender & P. J. McLaughlin's *The tough kid professional development teleconference series,* University of Georgia, Athens, GA.

## Chapter 3

# The Explosively Violent Kid

Gregory Clinton
William N. Bender

## *Why Do Some Students Explode?*

As discussed in the last chapter, aggressive behavior is usually highly tractable and very often predictable. Generally, most students with aggressive tendencies are known to be aggressive; in other words, they are predictably aggressive—and teachers are not taken back in surprise when aggression occurs from these kids. Most teachers anticipate verbal or even physical aggression from these students, and the wise teacher will be prepared in advance with an array of strategic ideas to defuse the situation and to decrease the aggression over the long term.

In contrast, some students seem to be only occasionally aggressive, and this aggression seems to be totally unpredictable. Further, these students can be extremely aggressive during those occasional episodes—posing a serious danger to themselves and others in the classroom. If placed in a special education class, these students may seem to move along for days or even weeks at a time, until the teacher begins to wonder what specific behavioral problems led to their identification and placement in the special education setting. Of course, when one least expects it, these students will seem to explode into verbal and/or physical violence. For example, the teacher may turn his or her back for only a minute, and in that brief time, a student will shout out a string of obscenities and throw a punch at the kid at the next desk.

Because of this unpredictability, the explosively aggressive student may be one of the most difficult types of problem students to manage. The totally unpredictable nature of his or her behavioral outbursts may create an overall uneasiness on the part of the teacher, who may find himself or herself dreading the beginning of that particular class each day.

> Because of unpredictability, the explosively aggressive student may be one of the most difficult types of problem students to manage.

Of course, the explosively aggressive student will tend to suffer more from social isolation than students with other problems, since both students and teachers strongly prefer people whose behavior is, at the very least, predictable. To illustrate this, one need only consider an aggressive child whose aggression is constant and predictable. Although some social isolation is likely in that case, there may be times when the child is a "preferred" playmate, such as on the touch football field at recess. In the case of touch football, some aggression is appropriate and may be desired by one's teammates. However, even in that situation, the explosively aggressive child will tend to suffer social isolation from his or her peers. The explosively aggressive child, then, probably suffers more social isolation than children with any other behavioral symptoms.

Further, the chronic extremes of behavior demonstrated by these students greatly limits the available disciplinary options that the teacher may employ. Of course, the diffusion tactics described in the last chapter are very appropriate for this type of student as well as the constantly aggressive student. However, the traditional behavioral strategies—many of which work quite well in other contexts—may in this context only result in charting appropriate behavior for five to six days and then attempting to intervene in one extreme behavioral eruption. From an intervention perspective, what can a teacher really do with that charted data?

Likewise, given the unpredictable nature of these students, the peer confrontation strategies described previously may merely exacerbate the problem. The student may be accepting of the analysis of his or her behavior by the class, until a certain student—either a friend or foe—contributes to that discussion. At that point, an explosion may occur, which the teacher then has to handle immediately because of the violence potential.

> If a teacher begins to carefully tune in to an explosive student, he or she can be quite sensitive in detecting aggressive eruptions prior to their occurrence.

*Billy leaves the room.*

What, then, can a teacher try with these explosive students? A moment's reflection on the type of problem behavior described may shed some light on this answer. Specifically, most experienced teachers can recall having taught this type of explosive student, and many teachers can recall knowing that a student seems ready to "explode" from the moment he or she entered the classroom on a particular day. On those days, teachers may find themselves treading lightly around the student in an effort not to trigger the explosion that they anticipate. In fact, if a teacher begins to carefully tune in to an explosive student, he or she can be quite sensitive in detecting aggressive eruptions prior to their occurrence. Of course, veteran teachers have learned to do this routinely. This heightened awareness of the pending explosion, even before something in the classroom triggers it, can allow the teacher to intervene effectively with the student. However, for explosive/aggressive kids, the teacher must have established one of several possible interventions prior to any particular explosion on any particular day.

In the same way that a teacher can determine that the student seems to be explosive on a particular day, the student can likewise be trained to make the same determination, and that can result in the development of powerful interventions. Students of this type do not respond well to many behavioral interventions (e.g., token economies or response cost), but they usually do respond well to interventions that result in empowering them to get a better handle on their own behavior. Most explosive children realize that their unpredictable behavior is doing harm to them socially, and most will be motivated to get a better handle on their own behavior. Thus, these students can become motivated allies of the teacher in curbing their own behavior.

This chapter presents two very different interventions that result in empowering a student to sense and forecast his or her own behavioral outbursts. From the relational discipline perspective, the teacher will serve in a supportive relationship role with the child when using these several strategies. The *relaxation strategies* have been used with explosively aggressive kids for several decades, and the common element in the variety of relaxation strategies is the sense that these kids can gain control of their own explosive behavior, rather than letting it continue to control them. Likewise, the application of an *adult mentoring* program, such as those described in the latter section of this chapter, can have the effect of providing a release for the tension these students seem to demonstrate, as well as an opportunity for positive reflection on their behavior. Using either of these intervention tactics, explosive students will feel empowered and valued in the planning and implementation of the intervention. With these two interventions in place in the classroom, the experienced teacher will be in a position to deal with these children.

## Chill-Out Ideas: The Relaxation Tactics

> Children must be taught about their explosive behavior in a fashion in which they perceive that they are gaining control over the behavior.

The term *relaxation/body awareness tactics* is used to describe a set of techniques that help a child gain increased control of a seemingly uncontrollable behavior. Any tactic that effectively relaxes a student, reduces tension, makes the student aware of and sensitive to stress, and thus provides a time for reflection on the rage that often underlies the explosive behavior may be considered a relaxation strategy. The reflective aspect of this strategy is crucial. Children must be taught about their explosive behavior in a fashion in which they perceive that they are gaining control over the behavior. The student's willing participation is also critical—the child must believe that he or she can "escape" from a behavior that has been quite destructive in his or her social life. In general, most explosively violent students, once they open up to the teacher and/or another significant adult, will state that they would like to get better control of these explosive tendencies. Thus, joint reflection on specific examples of explosive behavior is essential.

From the relational discipline perspective, this joint reflective time also builds quite an important bond between the student and the teacher. It is not uncommon for this type of bond to last for many years after the student has moved on to other classrooms or even graduated from school.

Of course, application of these tactics can be a time-consuming process. Still, effective use of these strategies is infinitely preferable to the alternative—allowing the student's uncontrollable and unpredictable behavior to set the atmosphere for the entire class for the entire year.

> The rationale for using relaxation tactics for explosively violent and/or aggressive kids is simple: Very few other strategies will work for this group of students.

The application of various relaxation approaches for explosively violent and aggressive kids has been common for the last two decades (Carter & Russell, 1985; Robin, Schneider, & Dolnick, 1976; Yell, 1988). Among the relaxation approaches that have been studied, one will find various exercise programs, specific relaxation training techniques, and even biofeedback. Some of these tactics are routinely applied in schools today, and research evidence does support the use of these tactics for a variety of children. The rationale for using relaxation tactics for explosively violent and/or aggressive kids is simple: Very few other strategies will work for this group of students.

## *The Turtle Technique*

Schneider (1974) and Robin (Robin, Schneider, & Dolnick, 1976) developed this particular self-control technique and were the first to demonstrate its effectiveness for young aggressive students with conduct disorders. Basically, the technique consists of several components, including the so-called turtle relaxation phase, a problem-solving phase, and peer support.

> Students are taught that they can decide on their own to do a "turtle" when they feel rage or anger, or teachers have a right to request that students do a "turtle" for a while.

*A student explodes!*

The technique first makes use of the "turtle" image—of withdrawing into one's shell or protective space when provoked by the external environment (Fleming, Ritchie, & Fleming, 1983). According to Robin and colleagues (1976), young children are taught to withdraw into their shells by placing their heads on their desks, locking their arms under their heads, and closing their eyes. They are told that this is how the turtle protects itself and draws strength to face the outside world. Students are taught that they can decide on their own to do a "turtle" when they feel rage or anger, or teachers have a right to request that students do a "turtle" for a while. While in the "turtle," the children are taught to relax their muscles in order to cope with emotional tensions. After a period of relaxation, the students begin a series of problem-solving tactics that allow them to reflect on their behavioral outbursts (Robin, Schneider, & Dolnick, 1976). The following dialogue illustrates how young aggressive children may be taught this technique:

### Turtle Teaching Dialogue
Little Turtle was a handsome young turtle very upset about going to school. He always got in trouble at school because he got into fights. Other kids

would tease, bump, or hit him: He would get very angry and start big fights. The teacher would have to punish him. Then one day he met the big old tortoise, who told him that his shell was the secret answer to all his problems. The tortoise told Little Turtle to withdraw into his shell when he felt angry and rest until he was no longer angry. So he tried it the next day, and it worked. The teacher now smiled at him and he no longer got into big fights. (Robin, Schneider, & Dolnick, 1976)

Beyond teaching the turtle response itself, two additional aspects of this technique should be emphasized. First, after the relaxation, the student is to engage in some reflective problem solving concerning his or her behavior (Robin, Schneider, & Dolnick, 1976; Fleming, Ritchie, & Fleming, 1983). For example, in the study by Fleming and colleagues, four basic problem-solving steps were taught to the students: (1) identify the problem, (2) generate alternative solutions, (3) evaluate alternatives and select the most appropriate, and (4) implement the selected alternative. Both group and individual applications of these steps should be practiced during the learning phase while students are beginning to use the turtle idea.

In fact, a class activity in which certain behavioral scenarios are discussed by the class can provide a very effective opportunity to analyze inappropriate behavior and brainstorm more appropriate behavior. Knapczyk (1988) used videotaped examples of junior high school students' aggressive behavior as a discussion point to initiate reflection on one's behavior, with positive results. Although these reflective, problem-solving strategies can be taught fairly easily, the teacher will need to spend some concentrated time on this problem-solving instruction.

Second, it is critical that the other members of the class respect the student's choice to become a "turtle" for a few moments. The class must be instructed not to talk to, joke with, or talk about the student who has chosen to withdraw into his or her shell. Support from the class, in the form or ignoring the student during his or her withdrawal, can make this technique very effective.

## Other Relaxation Tactics

Application of the "turtle" dialogue/metaphor itself should probably be limited to lower grades (i.e., grades K through 4), but alternatives using this basic idea are appropriate up through high school. For example, students in secondary school may be encouraged to place a sign on their desks that says "Time Out" when they need a break from the stress of the classroom envi-

Students in secondary school may be encouraged to place a sign on their desks that says "Time Out" when they need a break from the stress of the classroom environment.

ronment. In this case, the phrase *time out* does not mean application of the behavioral strategy of time out (i.e., absence of reinforcement). Rather, the phrase and sign indicate that a student needs a momentary escape from the academic and/or social demands of the classroom. The student should then place his or her head on the desk and peacefully relax for a few minutes. Teachers and students should agree not to call on or ask questions of the student while he or she is in this time out.

As another alternative in higher grades, audiotapes have been used in schools to foster relaxation. For example, a series of audiotapes by Lupin (1977) include 15-minute descriptions of imaginary trips to the beach and mountains. The sounds of these various environments are on the tape, coupled with a soft voice describing the scene in a fashion that is designed to foster relaxation.

## Biofeedback and Exercise

In addition to relaxation training itself, various other strategies have been used to assist in modifying aggressive behavior and other problem behaviors, including exercise programs and biofeedback (Christie, Dewitt, Kaltenbach, & Reed, 1984; Yell, 1988; Zenter, 1982). In each of these interventions, similar to the relaxation techniques just described, the student is provided with an opportunity to become more sensitive to stress in his or her body and to reflect on his or her aggressive behavior. Specifically, in both biofeedback and exercise, the student is increasingly focused on a sense of awareness of how his or her body is feeling (how he or she is relating to stress) and how he or she may control that stress without violent explosions.

For example, Yell (1988) was able to use a 30-minute warm-up and jogging/walking period with six students with behavioral problems and show a reduction in inappropriate classroom behaviors. The target behaviors for all six of the students (either talking out or out-of-seat behavior) were reduced during the jogging phases of this study.

Biofeedback has also been used to teach students to gain control over their own stress levels (Christie, Dewitt, Kaltenbach, & Reed, 1984). In biofeedback, a set of sensors designed to pick up the physiological signs of stress (i.e., the electrical resistance of the skin is one indicator of stress) is taped to a student's body. When the indicators of stress increase, an auditory tone increases in frequency. The child is told, during the biofeedback session, to "think about relaxing things that make the tone go lower." Thus, over a series of sessions, the student will subtly learn to reduce his or her level of stress. For explosively violent kids, this can equip them with the skills they need to foresee their own violent outburst and forestall it.

## Choosing the Right Relaxation Strategy

The choice of relaxation strategies may be determined in part by the situation. For example, for students in special education who live in large cities, implementation of biofeedback may be an option. The special education placement may provide a timely opportunity for this intervention, and if a biofeedback center is located near the school, such an intervention may be included on the child's individualized education plan, as it has been for some children with severe conduct disorders.

Still, this is very uncommon in schools today simply because biofeedback centers are fairly rare in most smaller communities. Also, this intervention will usually require transporting the child to the biofeedback center. Consequently, use of this option is rare, even though research has clearly indicated that this intervention works for many behavior problems (e.g., the most recent research on this technique has been the successful implementation for students with attention deficit hyperactivity disorders).

> Most teachers who wish to use a relaxation strategy opt for some version of the turtle technique, the relaxation audiotapes, and/or the time-out technique.

With this limitation in mind, the teacher must select from exercise programs, relaxation programs, or something like the turtle technique. Generally, exercise programs will take more time away from a student's academic study time, since dressing and postexercise showers may take up time beyond that required for the exercise. With that limitation in mind, most teachers who wish to use a relaxation strategy opt for some version of the turtle technique, the relaxation audiotapes, and/or the time-out technique mentioned earlier. As a practitioner, you should determine which techniques work for various explosive students, and use the technique that is most applicable in your classroom.

## One Caring Adult: Mentoring Programs

Mentoring programs have been widely implemented in recent years as dropout prevention programs and in curbing serious behavior problems, including explosive behaviors. *Mentoring* has been described as a one-to-one relationship between two people who are of different ages and are not relatives, whose relationship is formed to support the younger person through some aspect of development and is sustained over time (Flaxman, 1992). There are many factors that interact to put young people at risk for developing explosively aggressive or violent behavior, and it is clear that a caring adult who is available to a child over time can positively influence the direction of that child's development (Katz, 1997). Adult mentors, in addition to offering support for children in crisis, often provide a base for sustained reflection on one's behavior, and such reflection can assist students who have explosive tendencies.

### Initial Thoughts on Mentoring

Chapter 1 presented one rationale for mentoring (i.e., appropriate behavioral role modeling), but there are several additional arguments for this

*Adult mentoring works!*

approach. First, mentorships generally work regardless of the similarities or differences between the mentor and his or her charge. However, mentorships seem to work more effectively when the mentor and the student have a great deal in common. For example, psychologists have recently emphasized the critical influence of a same-sex role model to assist children in becoming successful adults (Warshak, 1992), and his same-sex factor should be attended to when possible. Also, some mentorship programs emphasize the importance of race in selecting mentors. Thus, if possible, one should use an African American male for an African American male child. This is the thrust behind the 100 Black Men of Atlanta and other similar groups in various large cities—African American males spending some time each week mentoring African American boys that are at risk for behavior problems.

This need for similar mentors points to a rarely discussed problem in education today: a lack of male role models in schools. Over 85 percent of all teachers (the percentage is much higher in the lower and elementary grades) are female, and well over two-thirds of the children referred for overt behavior problems are male. The federal government has noted that a disproportionate number of kids in special education come from single-parent households—where men are typically excluded. Statistics such as these do not suggest overt bias, but the clear reality is that more men are desperately needed to serve as mentors in the lives of this nation's male children (Pollack, 1998, pp. 1–12). In fact, one could argue that the country has inadvertently created schools in which males will fail disproportionately, because of this lack of male role models. If there is no male in the male child's home environment, and schools have few male teachers in classrooms, the only remaining way for a young boy to learn how to be a successful man would seem to be this year's version of a *Rambo* movie (i.e., violence is the correct response to every conflict).

What would society's response be if these figures were reversed—if 85 percent of teachers were male, if the majority of divorces led to the absence of a mother, and if 75 percent of kids identified for behavioral problems were female? Would not this be perceived as discrimination against females? As these questions indicate, more men are needed in the nation's classrooms; the disciplinary and role model needs of male students in schools simply demand it. Perhaps adult mentorship programs can, in part, address this need.

It should also be noted that mentorships work regardless of the "teaching" that goes on in the mentorship. In other words, some school-based mentorships are structured, at least initially, around tutoring, but most effective mentorships move beyond this interaction into the interest areas or hobbies of the kids and the mentors. This fact can explain what is significant about the mentorship: It is not the "content" around which a mentorship is structured, but the *relationship* between the mentor and the student that is all important. For these reasons, implementation of this adult mentorship strategy can be an important tool in alleviating disciplinary problems.

Getting an adult mentoring program off the ground can be quite a challenge, however. Asking the right questions is essential at the beginning stage. Following is a list of key questions for you to consider in your initial planning:

### Key Questions in Adult Mentoring*

- What problems need to be addressed? For example, does the school have a high dropout rate? Is there a high teenage pregnancy rate? Are students overtly aggressive in particular classes or in particualr areas of the school?
- Which students will participate? How many? Does a particular elementary or secondary class need help? Or does a special population (e.g., learning disabled, physically disabled, pregnant teens, etc.) need help? The target population will, to a great extent, determine the number of mentors needed and the role they should play.
- How will the program be led and coordinated? Without good leadership and coordination, any mentoring program is bound to fail.
- What resources can be utilized from the school? Is a classroom available for this program? Is a teacher available on a part-time basis to coordinate it?
- What existing mentor programs are similar in focus such that they can serve as models? It is useful to examine exemplary programs that have served students similar to the students you are endeavoring to reach.
- What funding sources are available? Consider Title I funds, state grants, PTA/PTO, Kiwanis Club and other community service organizations, and corporate foundations.

A number of sources provide information on mentoring programs (Benard, 1992; Clinton & Miles, 1999; Flaxman, 1992; Flaxman and Ascher, 1992; Freedman, 1991; Hamilton & Hamilton, 1992; Reilly, 1992; Smink, 1990; Sonsthagen & Lee, 1996), though specific instructions can be difficult to find. The following 10 steps represent a summary from these various sources.

---

*Adapted from *Violence Prevention and Reduction in School* (p. 37) by W. Bender, G. Clinton, and R. Bender (Eds.), 1999, Austin, TX: Pro-Ed. Adapted by permission.

## 1. Identify and Select Program Staff

A steering committee or advisory board—comprised of school staff, parents, business representatives, community leaders, and perhaps students—may be set up as the mentoring program's governing body. These persons represent the stakeholders in the project, and their input, particularly for districtwide programs, is essential. However, within the school, one mentorship coordinator should be assigned to oversee the day-to-day progress of the program and to be available to participants whenever problems occur. If possible, this should be more than a volunteer position—it should be strengthened by a monthly stipend plus some allotment for expenses. This will help not only to meet program needs but also to promote longer tenure in the position and thereby increase program stability. In some cases, a veteran teacher may be relieved from instructional responsibilities for half a day, and that person could coordinate the mentorship program.

## 2. Establish Program Goals

Well-articulated program goals, centering on building youth competence in some way, reap a benefit on two levels. First, a mentoring effort that is driven by clear goals will run more smoothly administratively. Clear goals help keep administrative decision making in focus, thus avoiding "mission drift."

> A common interest is the stuff from which friendships are made, and a desirable interpersonal relationship is more likely to grow out of a focus on working toward a goal than from a focus on building a relationship.

Second, clear and achievable goals for the program translate into clear and achievable goals for the mentoring partners. For example, the mentor and the student might improve certain academic or career skills or develop a commonly chosen hobby. Thus, the mentoring team is given a structure, a common task at hand, that gives the relationship "something to grow out of." A common interest is, after all, the stuff from which friendships are made, and a desirable interpersonal relationship is more likely to grow out of a focus on working toward a goal than from a focus on building a relationship (Hamilton & Hamilton, 1992). Moreover, having this structure provides both partners with an understandable purpose for their involvement, which can be a key factor in predicting regularity of meetings (Hamilton & Hamilton, 1992). Other examples of program goals might include:

- To decrease the likelihood of aggressive behavior by students with behavioral problems
- To provide male adolescents at risk for dropping out of school with male mentors in order to increase the students' attendance, academic achievement, and motivation to complete school

> Without well-written objectives as guideposts, program coordinators will lack direction in their work and have no clear means of reporting back to their steering committee what has been accomplished.

For each program goal, there should be a set of measurable objectives. Specific, concrete objectives are needed to provide the program with a way to assess progress toward reaching its goals. Without well-written objectives as guideposts, program coordinators will lack direction in their work and have no clear means of reporting back to their steering committee what has been accomplished, or of knowing what the committtee is looking for in such a report.

Several objectives should typically be listed under each goal, and each should specify a time frame. Some objectives should be designed so that they can be met early in the year, with others in the middle, and some at year end (One on One Foundation, 1991). Following is a list of sample objectives:

### Sample Objectives for Adult Mentoring*

- By the fourth week of the mentor recruitment/training period, 30 volunteer mentors will have been screened and enrolled in the program.
- By the October 1 launch date, all mentor/student pairs will be assigned.
- By the seventh week, 9 out of 10 students will have attended 80 percent of their meetings with mentors.
- By the ninth week, 8 out of 10 students will have mastered the first vocational skill area assigned (e.g., job application forms).
- By the ninth week, each mentor will report having at least one in-depth conversation with his or her student about choosing alternatives to violence in specific situations.
- By the end of the first year, elementary students will have increased their reading proficiency by one grade level.

*Adapted from *Violence Prevention and Reduction in School* (p. 38) by W. Bender, G. Clinton, & R. Bender (Eds.), 1999, Austin, TX: Pro-Ed. Adapted by permission.

- By the end of the first year, incidents of aggressive or violent behavior involving students in the program will have decreased by 40 percent.

Bear in mind that some of the benefits you seek most for student participants will be rather intangible (e.g., wanting them to find more meaning in life, to become more resilient, and to begin recognizing a wider set of solutions to problems). These can never be measured as accurately as one would like, but questionnaires and/or interviews can be used to gather evidence of improvement, and results on these can be incorporated into program objectives.

> Some of the benefits you seek most for student participants will be rather intangible (e.g., wanting them to find more meaning in life, to become more resilient, and to begin recognizing a wider set of solutions to problems).

### 3. Prescribe Activities and Procedures

Mention has already been made of the need for mentoring partners to have an activity they can pursue together, to provide a basis for the relationship to grow. This activity should be determined by the goals of the program. If the primary goal is academic improvement, some form of tutoring is most appropriate. If reduction of violence or aggressive behavior is the goal, common interest in a particular hobby may provide a nonthreatening framework that will allow the mentor to engage the youth in reflective conversations about choices and values. If the relationship "takes hold," hopefully the weight of the mentor's influence can make a difference in this area.

Procedures for mentors will also need to be clarified at this point. You will need to determine the kind of relationship you anticipate between mentoring partners and to develop guidelines for mentors. Sample guidelines follow:

#### Mentor Guidelines*
- Call the school to find out if the student is present. If your student is absent, you may assist in the classroom during the mentoring period.
- Sign in at the school office when you arrive at school.

---

*Adapted from *Violence Prevention and Reduction in School* (p. 39) by W. Bender, G. Clinton, & R. Bender (Eds.), 1999, Austin, TX: Pro-Ed. Adapted by permission.

- Pick up the student from his or her classroom, checking with the teacher concerning any special events you may need to be aware of. Proceed to the Mentoring Center.
- If there is a time when you would like to give your student a special gift, the gift should be small, be inexpensive, and serve as a reward for a job well done.
- All information (test scores, behavior, family, etc.) regarding students is confidential. Discuss all concerns about confidentiality with the mentor coordinator.
- Monthly meetings are held the second Wednesday of the month at 4:30 in the Mentoring Center to discuss achievements, concerns, plans, etc.
- Training sessions for new mentors will take place during regular monthly meetings. You can invite others to participate and come in with you.
- All mentoring sessions will be held on school campus during regular school hours. If you choose to undertake an off-campus trip or some activity after school hours, you must arrange that with the parents of the child. Such activities are not to be considered a part of the mentorship, and you will have legal responsibility for the child during those activities.

Questions such as when, where, and how long to meet, how much flexibility there is in meeting times, assigned activities, family contact policy, and what is expected by students should be addressed clearly for mentors during early training. This information should be provided in written form, in a handout packet or handbook for the mentors. A calendar of scheduled activities should be included as well.

### 4. Identify Students

Students are generally voluntary participants in the mentoring program. They may be referred by teachers, their parents, school guidance counselors, social workers, or the court system. The type of student to be served should be determined carefully by the mentoring coordinator and/or the steering committee and incorporated into the stated program goals (Sonsthagen & Lee, 1996).

The primary issue in the selection of students is whether mentoring is appropriate for a particular student (e.g., perhaps a severely disadvantaged or troubled youth) or is best suited for the youth typically regarded as at risk, who could overcome his or her life circumstances with a little extra support (Benard, 1992). Program leaders must be aware that, if they want to serve the truly disadvantaged, they must plan for long-term, intensive mentoring and be ready to intervene when problems arise or relationships fail (Freedman, 1991). Generally speaking, mentoring programs that have been more successful have been those serving kids whose academic or behavioral problems are not too severe and whose cooperation with the program is not difficult to obtain (Flaxman & Ascher, 1992). This is a reasonable proposition considering the fact that most programs depend on adult volunteers who are not trained social workers or behavioral specialists.

Further, the volunteer mentors are the "currency" of the adult mentoring program. These volunteers must be cherished and treasured, since their participation will be wanted again next semester or next year. Consequently, using mentors for students with severe problems may not be your wisest choice. Students who can be explosively violent are difficult to manage in the traditional classroom but can be good candidates for mentorship programs, providing that careful consideration is given to the selection of the mentor (see the discussion below).

## 5. Recruit Mentors

Selection of adults for participation in a mentorship program must be done judiciously; it is not as easy a task as it may appear. Though simply finding enough volunteers can be quite a challenge, some screening is needed of potential mentors to assure that unsuitable applicants are eliminated during the recruitment process. Two critical concerns involve the seriousness of the applicants' time commitment and whether their expectations are realistic. Applicants need to be informed about the hard realities of mentoring from the beginning so that only the truly committed ones will choose to continue with the program (Freedman, 1991).

> Any persons with a record of predatory behavior toward children should not be provided with the kind of ready access to individual youths that mentoring affords.

In addition, protection of the children in their charge is always a responsibility of educators. For example, any persons with a record of predatory behavior toward children should not be provided with the kind of ready access to individual youths that mentoring affords. As an extra precaution after screening, some programs limit mentor/youth meetings to public places (Flaxman & Ascher, 1992).

As one mechanism for recruiting volunteers, you may precede your actual mentorship program with a description of the planned program in the local newspaper. An article such as this could serve as a discussion point for presentations to local organizations about the proposed program.

Major businesses should generally be approached separately. Also, if you already have a commitment from a major business or two, be sure to include this in the concept write-up, unless you believe this would interfere with the commitment of other businesses still being courted. Involvement in education, and in mentoring in particular, is in the best interest of the business community; therefore, do not hesitate to approach these constituents of the wider community served by your school.

For the opening of recruitment, be sure to have announcements ready in several media so that radio, newspaper, fliers, posters, and any other media (such as e-mail or websites) begin at the same time and reinforce each other in the public eye. Look for natural channels for word-of-mouth promotion of the opportunity. Following are several additional suggestions for recruiting mentors:

### Methods for Recruiting Volunteers*

- Hold an open house in a central location in the community. Bring top people from the schools and from organizations to discuss the program with potential mentors.
- Advertise in local newspapers and on local TV and radio stations. Provide success stories to the local press for publication.
- Advertise in local university and college newspapers and on bulletin boards in different departments. Most fraternities and sororities have requirements to participate in community service projects, and their members may be interested in mentoring.
- Invite the aid of the religious community. Program coordinators should discuss program goals with members of the clergy and solicit their help in seeking mentors.
- Bring an experienced and enthusiastic mentor to recruitment meetings.
- Arrange for program coordinators to meet with small groups of potential mentors and/or sponsors to discuss the program.
- Cultivate the support of volunteers who will be able to recruit their colleagues.

*Adapted from *Violence Prevention and Reduction in School* (p. 40) by W. Bender, G. Clinton, & R. Bender (Eds.), 1999, Austin, TX: Pro-Ed. Adapted by permission.

- Design an attractive and informative program description for display in advertising, including placement on bulletin boards throughout the facilities of companies or organizations.
- Provide companies, organizations, and newspapers with a press release about the program.
- Arrange to have special displays in company or school cafeterias.

Once you begin to receive inquiries, you will need an application form to give to volunteers. This application form will serve as the front end of the screening process and will include a release form authorizing receipt of criminal record information, on an annual basis, from any law-enforcement agency (see Figure 3.1).

The remainder of the screening process will take place as you begin to train volunteers and orient them to the realities of mentoring and the nature of the commitment you are seeking. As you move through the recruitment and training period, usually from two to six weeks in length, begin meeting with volunteers individually either to confirm their enrollment or to explain why you feel the job of mentoring is not a good fit for them.

### 6. *Train Mentors and Students*

In order for mentoring to be effective, both mentors and students must be prepared adequately for the experience. Mentors, in particular, should have certain basic issues clarified during initial training sessions, after their commitment to the program has been secured. To begin with, they need to understand the nature of the mentoring relationship itself (e.g., how "close" it is expected to be or not be, what involvement with the child's parents/ home life is anticipated, what costs are involved, and what happens if the relationship doesn't develop as expected). Mentors also need to be shown effective ways to work with parents; they need to hear from veteran mentors; and they need comparisons of communication styles between adults and youth (One on One Foundation, 1991). Program leaders can also assist new mentors greatly as well as further the goals of their program by acquainting mentors with the wider resources and services available to the youths. Such resources might include career information offered by the school guidance office, community youth recreation programs, or simply the variety of learning opportunities at the local library.

Volunteers should be required to attend two or more training sessions. These sessions should be designed to acquaint mentors with the realities of what they are volunteering to do. Session presentations should be positive and convey enthusiasm, and they should emphasize the rewards, rather than the demands, without glossing over the possibility of problems.

**FIGURE 3.1   *Mentor Application Form***

## Mentor Application Form

(PLEASE PRINT)                                                    Date:_____

**Name:** Dr./Mr./Mrs./Ms._____ **Age:** _____

**Mailing Address:** _____

_____

City: _____  Zip: _____

**Phone (H):** _____  **Phone (W):** _____  **Fax:** _____

**Employer:**_____

**Education** (check highest level):
High School__  Some College__  Associate Degree__  Bachelor's__  Master's__  Doctorate__

**Community Involvement:**_____

_____

**Experiences in Working with Children:**_____

_____

**Interest** (please check):

| | | |
|---|---|---|
| Travel ____ | Crafts ____ | Shopping ____ |
| Reading ____ | Art ____ | Cooking ____ |
| Walking/Hiking ____ | History ____ | Gardening ____ |
| Nature ____ | Science ____ | Collecting ____ |
| Music ____ | Computers ____ | Wildlife ____ |

Sports (specify) _____

Other _____

**Foreign Languages?** _____

**Preferences:**

Elementary (5–11 years old): ____  Middle (11–14 years old): ____  High (14–18 years old): ____

Age: ____  Gender: ____  Ethnic Group:_____

Personality of Student: _____

**I am willing to commit to at least 3 hours per month for the remainder of the school year.**

_____
(Applicant's Signature)

**In order to help the school match you with a child, please write a paragraph about yourself.**

_____
_____
_____
_____

Volunteers should receive a mentor handbook or packet. The training sessions can then be organized around the contents of this handbook, with other agenda items added as needed. Program leaders, ideally with the help of experienced mentors, can take turns presenting and generating discussion on the various items in the handbook and their intended use, taking time especially on mentor guidelines and tips for relating to parents. Role-playing is also a desirable component for the sessions, as is any visual enhancement you may be able to add, such as photos from previous mentoring activities, slide shows, or video presentations on mentoring. Other tips for training include the following:

### Tips for Training Mentors*
- The training site should be pleasant, conducive to learning, and centrally located; refreshments should be provided.
- Consider bringing experienced mentors together in a "mentor panel" to share their experiences with the trainees and to stimulate the discussion.
- Volunteers should be organized into small working groups of about five persons each, including a trainer in each group, to facilitate maximum participation of trainees.
- To keep the program interesting, trainers should not lecture at length but should use a variety of learning techniques, such as role-playing, slides and films, and training manuals.
- Training sessions should help the mentors enhance their existing skills as well as learn new ones.
- During practice sessions, trainees should receive feedback on how they are doing.
- A list of suggested activities for mentoring pairs should be provided during training, with some discussion of what materials and supplies are available.
- At the end of the sessions, mentors should complete a course evaluation form.

The students selected for the mentorship program will also need some degree of orientation to the mentoring concept and experience. They need to be aware of what to expect from the mentoring relationship, including many of the same issues that must be covered with mentors, such as mentor involvement with parents, where and when to meet, and whether (or how much) the mentor will be expected to spend any money on treats or other

*Adapted from *Violence Prevention and Reduction in School* (p. 44) by W. Bender, G. Clinton, & R. Bender (Eds.), 1999, Austin, TX: Pro-Ed. Adapted by permission.

items. Students will also need to understand the nature of their part of the commitment to meet together, in order to get the most out of the program.

Initial student training can be accomplished generally in a single orientation session, although you may wish to conduct follow-up meetings for the youths from time to time. Kids who have been involved in the program for the first year or more may subsequently be asked to participate in planning decisions for the following year. Additional suggestions for student orientation include the following:

### Student Orientation for Mentorship*
- Describe the purpose of the program and the reasons the students should want to participate.
- Discuss the potential benefits of participation (e.g., making a friend, improving in a subject, eventually gaining worthwhile employment, etc.).
- Discuss the limits of a mentor relationship. Students need to understand that the mentors cannot do everything for them, nor can they be surrogate parents.
- Explain the students' part in making the program a success (e.g., behaving courteously, keeping appointments, showing respect for mentors, etc.).

## 7. Provide Mentor Support

Not only do mentors need training but they also need ongoing support. Experienced mentor coordinators emphatically advocate supporting mentors and warn of the consequences of not doing so (Freedman, 1991). Mentors need to be able to compare notes with each other and hear ideas about approaches to try with activities. They need to be reassured that the mentorship coordinator is near and reachable, should problems arise. Also, they need to be recognized in some way for their efforts.

Monthly or bimonthly support meetings can be conducted initially by program leaders; some of these meetings may in time be turned over to experienced mentors. A calendar for these meetings should be incorporated into the initial handbook, or, alternatively, you may wish to develop this schedule during initial training, with input from the volunteers. A public recognition event, usually a dinner, should also be included in the master schedule. The acknowledgment of the mentors' contribution provided by this kind of event should also be supplemented throughout the year by notes or tokens of appreciation from teachers, administrators, and parents.

*Adapted from *Violence Prevention and Reduction in School* (p. 44) by W. Bender, G. Clinton, & R. Bender (Eds.), 1999, Austin, TX: Pro-Ed. Adapted by permission.

## 8. *Match Mentors and Students*

Finding a good match between mentor and student should be a major concern for any program coordinator. Mentoring relationships that do not "connect" or catch on, for whatever reason, and result in withdrawal by the youth or the mentor (or both), do damage to the morale of both participants. Youths who have become candidates for mentoring are often very familiar with being let down by adults, and they do not need yet another disappointment. Adult volunteers, on the other hand, can become jaded toward problem youths and be turned off from future participation as mentors.

> The matching process should be flexible enough to allow a change of partners if a pair does not work out.

The task of matching mentors and youths involves two primary issues: the degree of choice afforded to the participants and the degree of similarity between the mentor and the student in terms of race/ethnic background, gender, and class. There are no clear data about whether giving participants more opportunity to choose their partner makes a difference in terms of outcomes, though most programs include this feature. Most programs use questionnaires or profiles, completed by both mentors and students (or by mentors and students' teachers), as a basis for assigning pairs. Some programs use social events to allow the pool of youths and mentors to become acquainted, and then ask each individual to list persons with whom they would like to be paired. In any case, the matching process should be flexible enough to allow a change of partners if a pair does not work out.

Whether to match mentor and student by same race/same sex should depend first on program goals. Some programs, for example, are set up specifically to provide black male role models for inner-city black youths. Most school-based programs, on the other hand, are set up to serve any youth who can especially benefit from a mentor. Moreover, these programs often will not have an even match of characteristics between available mentors and qualifying students.

The literature suggests that, in general, program coordinators need only avoid what might be called "excessive" social or socioeconomic distance between mentor and student (Benard, 1992). Cross-race or even cross-gender pairs may not always be the ideal, but these mentors can still bond with and be quite beneficial to the youths, especially if the socioeconomic distance is not too great. Also, bear in mind that some socioeconomic difference is desirable, as a means of expanding the horizons of the youth. Although a mentor from outside the student's daily world will not readily comprehend the realities of that world, this does not prevent the adult from being a good mentor (Flaxman, 1992). It is the caring attitude of the adult that matters most. In the meantime, cross-race mentoring itself can bring the added benefit of building appreciation for cultural diversity—a desirable outcome that is certainly compatible with the mentoring ideal.

For students with explosively violent tendencies, additional care in matching mentors and students should be exercised. From the relational discipline perspective, the rationale for undertaking a mentoring program is to provide to an array of explosive kids (as well as kids with other types of problems) an opportunity to bond with a significant adult. Clearly, for explosive children, consideration should be given to the disciplinary style and disciplinary flexibility that a particular mentor is likely to demonstrate when explosions occur. The mentor for this type of student should be a strong, firm disciplinarian who is not threatened by behavioral outbursts but can lovingly contain them. Thus, this type of mentor can model for the student an ability to control one's own behavior. As the intimate relationship is established, the mentor can help the student reflect on his or her behavior and consider other behavioral options for situations in which the student's rage builds up.

### 9. Monitor Mentoring Process

> Reports become the primary means of tracking the progress of each mentoring relationship and of the program as a whole.

After each encounter between mentor and student, the mentor should fill out a brief report sheet and turn this in to the program coordinator. These reports become the primary means of tracking the progress of each mentoring relationship and of the program as a whole. The information provided by report sheets may also be supplemented by feedback from mentors shared during monthly meetings. The mentorship coordinator should review this information on a continuous basis in order to address problems as they occur and to make reassignments if necessary. The coordinator must also be prepared to make other services, such as counselors or social service agencies, available to the youth as needed.

### 10. Evaluate and Revise Program

A mentor evaluation questionnaire, used along with the reports of the mentoring sessions, will be helpful in determining each individual's quality of experience in the mentoring relationship, and will allow the mentorship coordinator to determine whether program goals and objectives are being reached. Depending on the age of the students participating, you might wish to consider also using a student questionnaire. These data will assist in revising the program at year end as well as during the first year of operation. At the end of each school year, you should compare actual experience with the stated goals and objectives of the program. Revisions will generally affect program procedures but may also take the form of adjustments in the program's goals and objectives.

## Conclusion

For students who are explosively aggressive, very few interventions are available, and obviously teachers will feel some degree of frustration. With the relational discipline paradigm in mind, the teacher must focus on strategies and tactics that will build an effective relationship with problem students. However, given the serious needs of explosively violent kids, perhaps the best that teachers can hope to accomplish is to find a method that will defuse the immediate trigger for the explosion (see diffusion tactics in the Chapter 2), while helping the child, over time, to become more aware of the negative effects of the explosive behavior. The relaxation tactics are quite useful in this regard.

Also, given the serious needs of these kids, an adult mentoring program may be the strategy of choice for explosive kids. An adult mentor can develop a relationship with a child in crisis and make that child feel valued. Further, the mentor can nurture a relationship that fosters reflection on the child's behavior. This would be the most desirable tactic for teachers to employ with these challenging kids.

## References

Benard, B. (1992). *Mentoring programs for urban youth: Handle with care.* Portland, OR: Western Regional Center for Drug-Free Schools and Communities, Northwest Regional Educational Laboratory.

Carter, J. L., & Russell, H. L. (1985). Use of EMG biofeedback procedures with learning disabled children in a clinical and an educational setting. *Journal of Learning Disabilities, 18,* 213–216.

Christie, D. J., Dewitt, R. A., Kaltenbach, P., & Reed, D. (1984). Using EMG biofeedback to signal hyperactive children when to relax. *Exceptional Children, 20,* 547–548.

Clinton, G., & Miles, W. (1999). Mentoring programs: Fostering resilience in at-risk kids. In W. Bender, G. Clinton, & R. Bender, (Eds.), *Violence prevention and reduction in school.* Austin, TX: Pro-Ed.

Flaxman, E. (1992, August). The mentoring relationship in action. *IUME Briefs, 3.*

Flaxman, E., & Ascher, C. (1992, August). *Mentoring in action: The efforts of programs in New York City.* New York: Institute for Urban and Minority Education, Teachers College, Columbia University.

Fleming, D. C., Ritchie, B., & Fleming, E. R. (1983). Fostering the social adjustment of disturbed students. *Teaching Exceptional Children, 15,* 172–175.

Freedman, M. (1991). *The kindness of strangers: Reflections on the mentoring movement.* Philadelphia: Public/Private Ventures.

Hamilton, S., & Hamilton, M. A. (1992, March). Mentoring programs: Promise and paradox. *Phi Delta Kappan,* 546–550.

Katz, M. (1997). Overcoming childhood adversities: Lessons learned from those who have "beat the odds." *Intervention in School and Clinic, 32,* 205–210.

Knapczyk, D. R. (1988). Reducing aggressive behaviors in special and regular class settings by training alternative social responses. *Behavioral Disorders, 14* (1), 27–39.

Loffredo, D. A., Omizo, M., & Hammett, V. L. (1984). Group relaxation training and parental involvement with hyperactive boys. *Journal of Learning Disabilities, 17,* 210–213.

Lupin, N. (1977). *Peace, harmony, awareness.* Hingham, MA: Teaching Resources.

One on One Foundation. (1991). *One on one: A guide for establishing mentor programs.* Washington, DC: U.S. Department of Education.

Pollack, W. (1998). *Real boys.* New York: Henry Holt & Company.

Reilly, J. M. (1992). *Mentorship: The Essential guide for schools and business.* Dayton, OH: Ohio Psychology Press.

Robin, A., Schneider, M., & Dolnick, M. (1976). The turtle technique: An extended case study of self-control in the classroom. *Psychology in the Schools, 13,* 449–453.

Schneider, M. (1974). Turtle technique in the classroom. *Teaching Exceptional Children, 7,* 21–24.

Smink, J. (1990). *Mentoring programs for at-risk youth: A dropout prevention research report.* Clemson, SC: National Dropout Prevention Center, Clemson University.

Sonsthagen, L. L., & Lee, S. (1996). America's most needed: Real life heroes and heroines. *Schools in the Middle, 5* (3), 37–42.

Warshak, R. (1992). *The custody revolution. New York:* Poseidon Press.

Yell, M. L. (1988). The effects of jogging on the rates of selected target behaviors of behaviorally disordered students. *Behavioral Disorders, 13,* 273–279.

Zenter, R. W. (1982). Psychological effects of a running program (doctoral dissertation, University of Oregon, 1981). *Dissertation Abstracts International, 42* (8), 3452A.

## Chapter 4

# The Clingy, Attention-Seeking Kid

Some children are overly clingy; they seem to need attention so badly that they absolutely exhaust every teacher with whom they come into contact. Some of these kids may panic if they are not allowed to sit next to the teacher at the desk or the teacher's worktable. In one sense, these students represent the attention tank phenomenon run wild! Of course, the relationship between the clingy child and the teacher tends to be negatively affected by this clingy behavior, since most individuals—teachers included—respond somewhat negatively to such demands on their time and attention. Thus, from the relational discipline perspective, an effective relationship is not built between the teacher and the clingy student, unless the teacher finds a way to address these attention needs of the child.

Every teacher has experienced clingy kids who seem to need more attention than others, but some kids are so demanding that their presence in the classroom may compromise the education of other students because they simply demand so much from the teacher. Early in the year, these children may situate themselves as close to the teacher as possible; they reach out and touch the teacher—in some cases pulling the teacher's clothes. They seem to demand the teacher's attention to such a degree that the teacher often feels drained at the end of the day. In some cases, these youngsters may be identified as having attention deficit hyperactivity disorder (ADHD); in fact, classroom misbehavior is so common among some ADHD children (see Bender, 1997, pp. 12–20, for a review) that some suspect many of those students misbehave in a tactical sense, specifically to gain attention from the teacher or the classmates.

They are more than willing to spend some time in time-out if their actions and antics receive the "approval" of laughter from the other kids in the class.

Alternatively, there are some students who get attention by performing for an audience in joking or distracting ways rather than clingy ways. These kids are always "on stage": They are the class clowns or class entertainers, and they are quite determined that their job is to amuse the audience. They are more than willing to spend some time in time-out if their actions and antics receive the "approval" of laughter from the other kids in the class.

Although the behavior of these kids appears to be quite different, the reason for the misbehavior is the same—the need for attention.

From the relational discipline perspective, the common denominator for these two types of kids' behavior is the overwhelming need for attention from someone. Although the behavior of these kids appears to be quite different, the reason for the misbehavior is the same—the need for attention. The attention tank phenomenon is quite apparent here, and these kids simply must have attention from either the teacher or the other kids in the class. The silver lining in this cloud may not be apparent; nevertheless, the desperate need for attention offers several practical and relatively easy solutions to managing these students. The strategies described in Chapter 2 (peer confrontation and responsibility strategies) will work with this type of child after he or she has reached the fourth or fifth grade, but there are several more gentle strategies that also work quite well across the various grade levels. Furthermore, these additional strategies can be somewhat easier to implement that either the peer confrontation or responsibility strategies.

The tactics presented in the remainder of this chapter are appropriate for students who need attention but obtain it in inappropriate ways. First, a strategy for younger, insecure, or clingy children is presented. Next, two strategies are offered that provide the child with the attention he or she needs so desperately: the Shine My Light tactic and the Video Monitoring strategy.

## Comfort for Clingy Kids: Classroom Structure

Effective teachers realize that how they structure their classroom has a profound effect on how students behave. For example, almost every experienced teacher who has the space will arrange the student's desks in a semicircle or horseshoe. When desks are arranged in that pattern, and a teacher is leaning over a student and helping with work, he or she is likely to be facing most of the rest of the class. Thus, visual monitoring of the behavior of the other students in the class is possible, and fewer behavioral problems are likely to result. Review the arrangement in Figure 4.1, and consider which students are still within visual range of the teacher if he or she works with particular students at various desks.

In addition to this room arrangement, there are several things that teachers in lower grades can do for the shy, clingy, or insecure student. Some of these suggestions are presented in the following list:

### Teaching Tips for Clingy Kids

- Present directions that are clear and concise and that require the students to establish eye contact with you while instructions are provided. Eye contact alone can serve to meet the attention needs for many kids.
- Create a predetermined signal with the class (e.g., clapping hands or turning off/on lights) that precedes giving directions. For younger

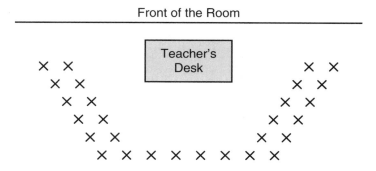

Note: Each **X** represents a student's desk, with 28 students in the classroom. In this arrangement, there are very few students who are not in the teacher's visual range at all times.

**FIGURE 4.1    *A Horseshoe Room Arrangement to Enhance the Teacher's Visual Monitoring of the Class***

kids who need special attention, you may wish to create a "special" signal just for them—for example, some type of hand gesture meaning, "I'm thinking of you, and I'll help if you need me!"

- Call the clingy student by name before giving instructions.
- Provide as many opportunities as possible for demonstration, hands-on activities, and/or use of manipulatives to reinforce more abstract concepts. In these demonstrations you can use the clingy kids as "assistants," thus providing them the attention they need.
- Provide the clingy student with appropriate opportunities to move around the room every 15 minutes or so (e.g., passing out papers, delivering attendance forms to the office, etc.), and make certain you interact with the clingy kid at each movement period. You may wish to praise him or her as an "excellent helper!"
- Structure instructional materials such that less desirable (i.e., less enjoyable) activities are followed by more desirable activities. Structure the activities such that the second activity is contingent on completion of the first activity.

*Clingy kids take time.*

- Keep a chart of the number of assignments the student completes each day. Throughout the day as well as at the end of the day make certain to praise the clingy kids for work completed.
- Assign shorter academic tasks to be completed, and provide reinforcement when finished (e.g., praise, smile, etc.).
- Provide reinforcement at various stages of completion for the clingy student (e.g., beginning, middle, and end of the task), since this gives him or her more contact with you.
- Reduce any emphasis on competitiveness that may cause the student to hurry his or her activities. Clingy kids tend to be somewhat insecure and usually do not respond well to competitive activities. However, they may "bloom" when offered a cooperative type of learning activity.
- Allow preferential seating in the front of the room or in close proximity to you to permit frequent eye contact.
- To the extent possible, limit distractions within the classroom. Allow the student to close doors or windows that might prove distracting.
- Keep the daily routine the same each day. Insecure kids who attach themselves to you will enjoy the structure of knowing what is going to happen in advance. Also, provide as pleasant and calm an atmosphere as possible.
- Maintain visibility of the student at all times.
- Activities requiring an active response pattern may be more helpful than those requiring a passive response, since this likely increases the contact that the clingy kid has with you.
- Allow time at the beginning of the day for organizing materials to be used during the day, and assist the child when necessary. This will lend additional structure to the class for the insecure kids.
- You may wish to assign "peer buddies" to work on various tasks together, and/or check on each other's readiness prior to beginning a lesson. This results in another student giving the clingy kid some attention (and, hopefully, you won't have to!).
- Remind the student at the end of the day about materials needed for the next day. This tactic helps a clingy kid sense the structure of the class.
- Establish with the student an individualized routine that he or she can follow each day (e.g., gather materials first thing in the morning). Clingy kids in the lower grades will draw some security from such routines.
- For independent seatwork, a quiet area (e.g., study carrel) may be helpful, particularly if other students are involved in more dynamic, inter-

active activities. Make sure the student understands that this is not a punishment.

- In the classroom, particularly in cooperative learning or other group activities, strive to surround the student with positive role models.
- Try placement in various instructional groups to determine which group seems to result in success for the clingy student.

> Choose the strategies, techniques, and suggestions that seem most comfortable to you.

Of course, a teacher would not try to implement all of these suggestions, but merely the ones that fit within his or her classroom management style. Thus, you should choose the strategies, techniques, and suggestions that seem most comfortable to you. Again, consider how each strategy you use affects your relationship with the child over the long term, as well as his or her relationship to the peers in the class.

## Make Me a Show-Off: The Shine My Light Strategy

In understanding the Shine My Light strategy, first recall from Chapter 1 one of the basic tenets of relational discipline: A kid who wants attention will get attention. Further, he or she will get attention from the person or persons whose attention is desired. These axioms are the basis of the attention tank phenomenon. If a particular student has a need for attention, the classroom simply must be structured in such a way as to meet that need. Otherwise, the student's attention needs will tend to predispose the class toward increasing harshness or even punishment, since the child will demand attention in inappropriate ways.

> Positive attention from classmates and the teacher assists in developing a positive self-image over the long term and thus tends to reduce behavioral problems.

### Self-Esteem and Behavior

One thing that teachers as well as parents can do to fill the need that some youngsters have for attention is to create ways for the kids to receive attention for positive accomplishments. Positive attention from classmates and

*Billy shining his light!!*

the teacher also assists in developing a positive self-image over the long term and thus tends to reduce behavioral problems.

When considering the factors that place some children at risk for poor behavior (problem home life, poverty, disabilities, etc.), the development of a strong, positive self-concept is perhaps the single-biggest factor in fostering resiliency of these kids. Although this book has not emphasized labels associated with different problems, students with learning disabilities and/or attention deficit hyperactivity disorder are particularly prone to lower than normal self-concepts (Franklin & Bender, 1997, pp. 227–252). Thus, these children often need assistance in strengthening their positive self-esteem. Consequently, if parents and teachers can subtly assist such a child in fostering a hobby, activity, or talent that can set the child apart from his or her peers, this may lead not only to increased self-concept but also decreased behavior problems and increased achievement.

Recall from Chapter 1 that in my consultant work with parents of students with ADHD, learning disabilities, or behavioral disorders, I have repeatedly asked what hobbies or activities the parents could assist the child to build into his or her life that would allow the kid to display a unique talent or knowledge that would make him or her feel like someone special In Chapter 1, I used flying as an example. Although flying is a relatively expensive example, I do not know of a single situation in which this tactic failed to work for an adolescent male with attention deficit hyperactive disorder. In that case, not only did the hobby of flying become something that the entire family began to enjoy together but also the academic demands of learning to fly (i.e., ground school and preparation for pilot exams) resulted in improved study habits and academic grades in academic subjects in school.

> Any hobby that gives a kid bragging rights to some special knowledge or skill may work to enhance self-esteem and provide positive attention for kids who need it.

However, even a relatively inexpensive hobby can be a point of great pride for a kid—it can provide an identity of which he or she is justifiably proud. For example, karate seems to be worshipped by today's youth; recall how many movies demonstrate the hero using this discipline during the climactic dual at the end. If cost is an obstacle, consider various self-defense classes taught at youth programs at the local YMCA. Again, any hobby that gives a kid bragging rights to some special knowledge or skill may work to enhance self-esteem and provide positive attention for kids who need it.

> A hobby can create an identity, and perhaps even a profession, if teachers and parents are carefully watchful and not overly forceful.

Caring parents as well as teachers will look for just this type of opportunity to give a child a hobby which in which he or she will grow. One recent hollywood hit (*October Sky*) focused on a caring teacher facilitating a student's interests in rockets, as an escape from the West Virginia coal mine. A hobby such as this can create an identity, and perhaps even a profession, if teachers and parents are carefully watchful and not overly forceful. Further, hobbies such as these let a kid who may otherwise seek attention in less than positive ways shine his or her light in a more acceptable way.

### Suggestions to Get Started

Parents as well as teachers can use this tactic by following a few simple guidelines. Parents may consider a wide array of options for finding a child a hobby or special skill. Teachers, on the other hand, are not able to facilitate getting a child to ball practice at the local recreation league or to the go-cart race track, for example, since these are typically after-school activities. However, teachers can and should encourage students to explore other areas of interest, and teachers may be able to influence children toward these areas. For instance, if a child shows an interest in painting, perhaps the teacher could assist in arranging a special visit or two by the art teacher. For a child with an interest in music, band may be a course that the teacher would want to recommend. An interest in karate, basketball, and/or automotive engines may be facilitated by careful selection of reading material for classroom work. The following guidelines will assist teachers and parents in this process.

> Teachers can and should encourage students to explore other areas of interest, and teachers may be able to influence children toward these areas.

### Identifying a Hobby for Personal Growth

- Observe the child from the early puberty years on up. A great deal of hobbies turn out to be short-term interests prior to puberty, but somewhere around the fifth grade, many individuals develop the interests and hobbies that stay with them for a lifetime. Watch closely but very subtly.
- Encourage the development of hobbies *covertly*, not overtly. Overt pressure from parents or teachers to develop a hobby can be quite destructive. For example, the teacher may merely mention to the student that the community has a soccer league for his or her age group, or the parent may offer instruction on safe camping (building fires, working with axes, selecting a spot for the tent, etc.). Almost any hobby will do, if it provides the child with something that he or she can demonstrate for others.
- Identify, if possible, a hobby that can be done relatively inexpensively and with other kids (e.g., shooting hoops in the side yard, tennis, stamp collecting, etc.).
- Identify hobbies that bring regular opportunities to show one's skill (e.g., dance recitals, science or social studies projects in school, musical performances, talent shows, etc.). The public performance of skills is the aspect that enhances self-concept.

> The teacher and/or parent should consider the subtle hints concerning what a student may wish to do as a hobby.

## A Planning Activity

In order to develop a list of options for a particular child, the planning sheet in Box 4.1 should be used. Note that the first part of the sheet involves collection of some information and observations on the child's attention-seeking behavior as well as his or her hobbies and interests. Also, in contemplating the use of this strategy, the teacher and/or parent should consider the subtle hints concerning what a student may wish to do as a hobby. How does the child spend his or her free time? Even video game preferences may provide subtle clues. For instance, does he or she prefer video games that challenge the mind with mysterious planning activities (*Mist* would be one example) or does he or she prefer sports games or flying spaceships?

Some kids misbehave in school by always being out of their seat, and, in some cases, this may involve regularly attempting to do specific tasks. Does the student stop his or her work and go to the computers in the back of the class for computer work or games? Does the student head for the VCR or other technology in the class, or does he or she go to the reading corner to find a particular type of book? Does the student complete assignments in science, or does the child choose to play in the science corner when he or she should be doing other tasks? These types of attention seeking misbehaviors can suggest particular areas in which a student is interested.

> Often, kids need only a small amount of encouragement to assist them in exploring fields of interest to them.

The next part of the planning guide involves noting ways to explore the identified areas of interest as well as any potential barriers to such exploration. Considerations here include the expense associated with the hobby and what resources are available within the school and/or the community. Clearly, resources that allow the child to explore a hobby or interest area are critical, and the planning guide (Box 4.1) will help you and the student explore options more completely prior to selecting something. Often, kids need only a small amount of encouragement along these lines to assist them in exploring fields of interest to them. You may wish to use the planning sheet with them on a periodic basis (perhaps once every six months) until a lasting hobby is found—one the child will do without prompting from the parent or teacher. Alternatively, the teacher and parent may use this form

**BOX 4.1** • *Planning Guide for Shine My Light Strategy*

### I. The Student's Behavior and Interests

Identify a student who has demonstrated attention-seeking, problem behaviors in the classroom. Consider the types of behavior that have been demonstrated.

1. Has this student shown aggressive or violent behaviors? Are those behaviors the most typical problem he or she demonstrates? If so, another procedure may be more appropriate (see Chapters 2 and 3).

   _____

   _____

2. Did the behavior result in laughter from the class? Was that the student's primary motivation?_____

   _____

3. Does the misbehavior itself suggest a particular task or a particular type of attention the child would like?_____

   _____

4. Does the child's interest show in his or her academic work in the class (e.g., a child who always writes stories about bicycles)?

   _____

   _____

5. What do others (e.g., parents and other teachers) say about the child's interests?_____

   _____

6. If asked, would the child identify areas of interest? _____

   _____

### II. Exploration Options

List below any options that seem to emerge from the analysis above, your reflections, and discussions with the child.

   _____     _____

   _____     _____

1. Which of these options are the least expensive?

   _____

*(continued)*

**BOX 4.1   Continued**

2. Are all of the options available, given the expense associated with almost any hobby?_____

_____

3. Which options take advantage of community resources (e.g., recreation leagues, ball fields, etc.)?_____

_____

4. Is some formal or informal training available to the child for any of these options (e.g., band training at school)?_____

_____

5. Can family and/or other students in the class provide some informal training in this area at no cost?_____

_____

6. Do these options offer regular opportunities for this child to demonstrate his or her newly acquired skill?_____

_____

together without the child present, to chart strategies to encourage the child to identify a hobby or skill that will let his or her light shine.

> Without some opportunity to demonstrate skill, the desired increases in self-esteem and resulting positive attention to the child are unlikely to materialize.

Once the questions of expense and available resources are answered, the final question must be considered: Does the student have ample opportunity to demonstrate his or her skill in the area of interest? Without some opportunity to demonstrate skill, the desired increases in self-esteem and resulting positive attention to the child are unlikely to materialize.

Of course, this does not mean that such demonstrations have to take place in the school environment. For example, if a child chooses a hobby that is not easy to demonstrate in school (e.g., scuba diving, camping, or flying), he or she could still be encouraged to demonstrate that skill in various science projects, photo and/or video projects, and other performance assessment demonstrations in an array of classes at school. This should result in attention for the child and the desired increases in self-esteem, and you will find that this simple tactic can alleviate numerous behavioral problems for many students.

## *Show Me: The Video Monitoring Strategy*

> The teacher's role must include teaching about the effects of one's behavior on one's relationships to others.

Many attention-seeking students with moderate conduct problems are not aware of the effect their behavior may have on others in the classroom. Of course, in relational discipline, the impact of behaviors on relationships is of paramount concern, and the teacher's role must include teaching about the effects of one's behavior on one's relationships to others.

> If subtle reactions from other class members could be demonstrated to the attention-seeking student, in many cases a positive behavior change would result.

As one example, some students who misbehave to entertain the class may not realize that their misbehavior is, quite often, cause for disdain or

*"Yes, I'm glad you're reading but . . . "*

even overt ridicule from their classmates. Although these junior comedians may believe that they improve their social status with their antics, the majority of their classmates may react quite negatively to the class clown, since the frequent classroom antics disturb the ongoing learning process. If these subtle reactions from other class members could be demonstrated to the attention-seeking student, in many cases a positive behavior change would result.

Some of these students deny that they have any behavior problems at all, and this denial can prohibit them from investing time in developing appropriate behavioral alternatives. Every experienced teacher has been faced with kids who, when spoken to after an overt misbehavior, look at the teacher with a "Who? Me?" expression on their innocent faces. These kids can be quite exasperating for most teachers.

Sometimes even family members of the misbehaving student will downplay the attention-seeking behavior problem. Often, during a conference with parents, teachers sense that their concern relative to the attention-seeking behavior is not shared by the parents. Many teachers have even had the experience of meeting with parents who pretend that no behavior problem exists, or even that the teacher is somehow "picking on" their child.

> Sometimes family members of the misbehaving student will downplay the attention-seeking behavior problem.

For these attention-seeking kids (and for some parents), a tactic called Video Monitoring may be of benefit, since this approach allows the teacher the option of showing the behavioral problem to both the student and his or her parents (Buggey, 1999). If a specific-attention seeking behavioral problem can be identified and defined in fairly specific terms, this strategy should be considered.

The Video Monitoring strategy calls a student's attention to his or her conduct problem in two mutually supportive ways: (1) charting the occurrence of the behavior problem and (2) using a television camera as a means of displaying the behavior directly to the student. The strategy depends on the joint application of these two documentation methods.

### When to Apply This Strategy

The Video Monitoring strategy is applicable for both boys and girls across the age span who demonstrate attention-seeking problems. In fact, like many techniques in this book, this tactic works for a wide variety of mild to moderate behavior problems, although this strategy is usually most effective when a student doesn't acknowledge that an attention-seeking behavioral problem exists. For example, students may feel that routine insults are comical for others in the class and may not realize the effect that these biting remarks have on other students. Thus, showing both the problem behavior and the resulting responses from others can help a student modify numerous behaviors in a positive way. Besides attention-seeking behavior, other behavior problems for which this strategy is effective include:

- Blurting out answers
- Interrupting other students
- Using rude or inappropriate language
- Name-calling
- Insulting other students
- Being verbally aggressive

Fairly consistent attention-seeking behavior problems that are likely to occur numerous times during a 35-minute instructional activity are the best candidates for this strategy.

The teacher should bear in mind that this tactic is not for every student or every type of misbehavior. Typically, this strategy should not be used for extreme behavioral problems, such as violent outbursts or constant fighting. In those cases, the student is not usually in denial about the effects of the behavioral problems, and other strategies would be more effective (see Chapter 2 for relational discipline strategies on aggression). Also, this Video Monitoring strategy is not particularly effective for low-frequency behaviors (i.e., those that occur only once or twice a week) for logistical reasons; it is very difficult to capture seldom-occuring behavior problems on video. Rather, the fairly consistent attention-seeking behavior problems that are likely to occur numerous times during a 35-minute instructional activity are the best candidates for this strategy.

### Video Monitoring Strategy Application

First, you, the teacher, must define the specific attention-seeking behavior(s) that is problematic or disruptive. Write down the definitions and include no more than two or three types of behavior for your intervention. You will be collecting frequency data on these behaviors during a specific period (perhaps the morning instructional period each day), and monitoring more than three behaviors becomes cumbersome. In fact, information on only *one* behavior is preferable.

After defining the behavior, you should obtain parental permission as well as permission from your administrator for videotaping the students in your class. In some cases, schools obtain a "universal" permission for videotaping all students at the beginning of the year. However, it is strongly recommended (and required in many school districts) that parental permission be obtained before videotaping begins.

Next, set up a video camera on a tripod to observe the student and several surrounding students. The camera should be perhaps 10 to 15 feet from the subject, and centered on the subject, but the view should also include perhaps one-fourth of the class members. A remote control is preferable for turning the camera on. Alternatively, you may merely let the camera run for the entire period of data collection (most VCR tapes will run for 6 to 8 hours) and capture on video all of the behaviors during that time. Of course, if you use this approach, you must review the tape in fast forward to find the video of the actual attention-seeking behaviors.

> Set up a video camera on a tripod to observe the student and several surrounding students.

On the first day the camera is set up and recording, begin a frequency count to record each occurrence of the problem behavior by the child. As a general rule, you should chart the occurrences of the behavior for four or five days. You will run the videotape on each day during this baseline period in order to capture good examples of the problem behavior.

> Merely inform the class that you are videotaping the effects of your instruction.

Note that, up to this point, you have not said anything to the misbehaving child about the camera, even though the class may have asked constant questions about it. Merely inform the class that you are videotaping the effects of your instruction. In most cases, the class will forget that the camera is rolling during the instructional period. After one or two days, they will be accustomed to it.

> Show several examples of the problem behavior to the student and share the frequency count you have compiled.

After a few days of videotaping, hold a conference with the student (and perhaps the student's parents) to discuss the attention-seeking behaviors that have been disrupting his or her (or other's) work. At that point, show several examples of the problem behavior to the student and share the frequency count you have compiled. Discuss with the student the specific behavior that you consider inappropriate and why it is disturbing to his or her work as well as to others in the class. Explain that the purpose of the camera is to capture on videotape each inappropriate behavior, for the teacher and student to review together.

> Imagine the impact if a class comedian sees other students looking bored or even disgusted with the behavior or comment that he or she thought was so funny!

The actual intervention begins the next day. You will hold a daily conference with the student and review the data and video examples collected on each behavior problem. Point out each example of inappropriate behavior to the child. Further, given the relational discipline emphasis on relationships, you should make a point to discuss with the student the impact of each attention-seeking behavior on the other members of the class. If you can capture an example of an attention-seeking behavior—perhaps a comment that the student thought was funny—and simultaneously capture a negative reaction from several other kids on the videotape, that can be a powerful motivator for behavioral change. Imagine the impact if a class comedian sees other students looking bored or even disgusted with the behavior or comment that he or she thought was so funny! In that sense, the Video Monitoring tactic forces the student to realize that his or her behavior is really an offense against the class and not merely an offense against the teacher.

Logistics must be considered here. Most teachers find that the daily conference will take approximately 15 minutes for the first two or three days. This time *must* be found after class in order for this tactic to work. Afterward, the time length of the daily conferences will decrease to as little as 5 minutes for succeeding days. Some teachers have found that a joint review of behavior every two days is as effective as a daily conference, but you should review the video together at least every two days at the beginning of the intervention in order to assure efficacy. After a period of time, you may wean the student to two conferences, and subsequently one conference each week.

During the first conference with the child, have the student identify a reinforcement that he or she will work for. Self-chosen reinforcements are quite often more effective than things the teacher may choose, but you should set some reinforcement parameters by offering a list of choices. Once a selection is made by the student, you should offer both daily and longer-term (i.e., once a week or so) reinforcement.

Box 4.2 peresents a brief synopsis of the steps for implementing the Video Monitoring strategy.

## Additional Adaptations

Like many tactics covered in this text, a number of modifications are possible with this strategy:

### Additional Applications and Modifications of Video Monitoring
- Share the videotape of the behaviors with special education teachers, the school psychologist, or other teachers of this student.

---

**BOX 4.2 • *Video Monitoring***

---

If a specific attention-seeking behavior can be identified, one effective strategy is to call the student's attention to the problem by (1) charting the behavior and (2) using a video camera as a means of displaying the behavior directly to the student.

*Strategy Application*
1. Define the specific behavior(s) that you consider to be the problematic or disruptive behavior(s).
2. Obtain permissions for videotaping, and then set up a video camera on a tripod to observe the student and surrounding students.
3. Begin a frequency count of each occurrence of the problem behavior.
4. After a few days, hold a conference with the student and show several examples of the problem behavior to the student. Also share the data with the student.
5. Intervention begins the next day. Hold daily conferences with the student and review the video of problems behaviors from that day. Point out the negative reactions from classmates, if any are noted on the video.
6. Have the student identify a reinforcement that he or she will earn by decreasing the behavior.
7. Wean the student from the daily conferences.

---

- If the child is likely to be embarrassed, consider hiding the camera in a cardboard box for filming.
- Assist parents in adapting this strategy to help the student understand how much time he or she spends off-task during homework.
- After several days of intervention, consider having the student count his or her own behavioral outbursts.

First, once a video is obtained of several examples of attention-seeking behavior, you might wish to share the videotape of the behaviors with special education teachers, the school psychologist, or other teachers of this student. Perhaps those professionals will want to try a similar strategy with this student in their class.

Second, if the student might be easily upset or embarrassed, consider hiding the camera in a cardboard box for filming. Although this can decrease the effectiveness of the strategy for some kids, it may be appropriate for others. Remember that the purpose of the camera is not to humiliate the student; the camera should be positioned to view a number of students, but only the student with the attention-seeking behavior will ever realize his or her behavior has been the subject of video observation.

Next, the Video Monitoring tactic can be useful with parents in at least two distinct ways. For instance, the videotape may help you convince reluctant parents that a behavior problem does indeed exist. Also, for parents who acknowledge a behavioral problem at home as well as at school, the strategy is very useful in home environments. Parents may adapt this strategy to assist a student in understanding how much time he or she spends off-task during homework periods, for example.

The fourth modification involves the child directly in monitoring his or her own behavior. You might consider having the student count his or her own behavioral outbursts from the videotape. You might even offer the student some reinforcement if his or her count matches yours.

Creer and Miklich (1970) implemented a video monitoring strategy that was the reverse of the tactic presented here. As an intervention for noncompliance and aggression, they videotaped a child's behavior and subsequently edited out all of the inappropriate behaviors. Then, by showing the video to the aggressive kids, they had a model of *appropriate and compliant* behavior rather than examples of inappropriate behavior. The results indicated that this technique worked to reduce the students' aggressive and noncompliant behavior.

As this example illustrates, there is a question concerning use of the videotape to show either negative or positive behavior. Whereas showing a student his or her inattentive behavior is probably worthwhile, experienced educators realize that modeling—including self-modeling—is an effective manner to teach behavior. Obviously, a teacher does not want to teach inappropriate behaviors using this technique, and it is possible that showing a child his or her inappropriate attention-seeking behavior may have that unwanted effect. However, for relatively minor behaviors, such as inattention and clinginess, showing the specific inappropriate behavior can be recommended, but for overt aggression and more serious behaviors, one should consider showing the child only appropriate behavior.

## Conclusion

The attention-seeking behavior of some kids can be quite disturbing to the class, and may be one of the most irritating aspects of teaching for the professional educator. Consequently, every teacher needs to command a series of tactics that can be used for attention-seeking kids. Each of the tactics presented in this chapter will allow the teacher to work with the student on his or her problem behavior, and should foster stronger relationships between the teacher and the child. Further, both the Shine My Light strategy and the Video Monitoring tactic focus on the child's relationships to his or her peers, and often results in a better understanding of those relationships by the attention-seeking child. With these strategies built into the regular classroom routine, you will be equipped to deal successfully with a wide array of attention-seeking behavior as well as other types of behavioral problems.

> Both the Shine My Light strategy and the Video Monitoring tactic focus on the child's relationships to his or her peers.

## References

Bender, W. N. (1997). ADHD at home and in the classroom. In W. N. Bender (Ed.), *Understanding ADHD: A practical guide for teachers and parents.* Columbus, OH: Merrill.

Buggey, T. (1999). "Look! I'm on TV!" *Teaching Exceptional Children, 31*, 27–30.

Creer, T. L, & Miklich, D. R. (1970). The application of a self-modeling procedure to modify inappropriate behavior: A preliminary report. *Behavior Research and Therapy, 8*, 91–92.

Franklin, L. M., & Bender, W. N. (1997). The adult with ADHD. In W. N. Bender (Ed.), *Understanding ADHD: A practical guide for teachers and parents.* Columbus, OH: Merrill.

## Chapter 5

# The Inattentive Kid

The type of youngster who tends to drive teachers to total frustration most easily and often is the inattentive student.

This book has presented a wide array of youngsters and youngsters' behaviors—among them have been defiant or aggressive kids, explosively violent kids, and kids performing for an audience. Although these students are certainly in-your-face kids, I have found that the type of youngster who tends to drive teachers to total frustration most easily and often is the inattentive student. Often, this type of student will demonstrate no overtly aggressive or violent behavior; in fact, in many cases, no behavior problems are noted at all, except an inability to remain focused on the schoolwork at hand. Of course, this inattentiveness leads to numerous academic problems, such as an inability to complete classroom work and, quite often, doing no homework. However, the child usually does not demonstrate any malicious or aggressive behavior, and, for this reason, teachers tend to like this type of child and want to find strategies to work with him or her. This is exactly what leads to the frustration on the part of the teacher—the fact that although this inattentive student is quite likable, no instructional strategies seem to work!

Of course, even in the absence of overt problem behaviors, an inattentive youngster can be quite disruptive to the class routine. Imagine, for example, a sixth-grade teacher, Ms. Thompson, teaching a unit on the solar system. She has the class fascinated—spellbound—with a model of the planets and various moons, as she discusses the rings around the outer planets. Suddenly, little Jake, from the second row, blurts out, "Ms. Thompson, I'm gonna get a go-cart for Christmas!"

Ms. Thompson may be inclined to wonder what happened. What type of mental connection did Jake make to get from the rings of the outer planets to his go-cart? What were the thought processes for that mental jump? Or, more plainly put, where is this strange kid coming from? Of course, the class is now quite taken with the disruption, and Jake doesn't even realize that he has done anything wrong!

Consider another example: After calming the class down and bringing Jake back to the task, another student—Jessica—gets excited when Ms. Thompson uses models of the planets. In fact, Jessica gets so excited that she begins to jump up and down in her seat several times, after which she rushes to Ms. Thompson and reaches up to touch the rings of Saturn, exclaiming, "That looks just like my basketball!"

> Jake and Jessica have demonstrated an amazing talent for interrupting the class with their inability to focus on the classwork, even when it is presented in an interesting fashion.

At this point, Ms. Thompson is quite frustrated; she can't get angry at these two students, as perhaps she would in the case of a violent or aggressive outburst, but she feels frustrated with having a successful lesson so disrupted. In actuality, Ms. Thompson has witnessed a very common phenomenon: inattention!

Both Jake and Jessica have demonstrated an amazing talent for interrupting the class with their inability to focus on the classwork, even when it is presented in an interesting fashion. Sometimes students such as Jake and Jessica will be identified as having attention deficit hyperactivity disorders, sometimes emotional disturbances, or behavioral disorders, and sometimes learning disabilities. Alternatively, this sort of student may have no identified disability at all, save a total inability to pay attention in class. Regardless of the label or lack thereof, this type of student can be particularly frustrating, simply because teachers want to assist them so very much. In fact, both Jake and Jessica may be among the brightest kids in the class.

> Attention problems are probably the single-biggest enemy of learning in today's classrooms.

*"Yes, Miss Jones, I took my medicine today."*

Upon reflection, attention problems of this nature are probably the single-biggest enemy of learning in today's classrooms. Specifically, the number of children identified with attention deficit hyperactivity disorders (ADHD) has skyrocketed during the last 10 years (Bender, 1997; p. 12). Estimates on the percentage of school-aged children with this disorder range from a low of 1 percent of the school population to a high of 23 percent, although most experts place the prevalence at around 4 percent. Many students with ADHD take prescription medications, but research has demonstrated that specific attention-building strategies can assist even those students receiving medications to increase their attention in class (Mathes & Bender, 1996).

> Almost every teacher in the public schools needs specific tactics that will assist children with attention problems.

Also, many children other than those identified with attention deficit hyperactive disorders demonstrate problems in attention; these include students with learning disabilities and behavioral disorders. These three groups together may include as much as 10 percent of the total school population. Given this many students with attention problems, almost every teacher in the public schools needs specific tactics that will assist these students regardless of the label.

This chapter will focus on two specific tactics that can assist a teacher in dealing with a child who is inattentive: self-monitoring of attention and application of group contingencies to enhance attention.

## Self-Monitoring of Attention

### What Is Attention?

> Since paying attention came as a fairly natural ability for most teachers, many assume that students know how to pay attention.

Teachers often tell inattentive students to pay attention in class; if there is one constant refrain from teachers across the nation it would be "Now, pay attention to this!" However, in spite of the attention problems demonstrated in the nation's classrooms, few teachers actually *teach* students exactly how to pay attention. Since paying attention came as a fairly natural ability for most teachers, many assume that students know how to pay

attention. This is, in a sense, understandable, because teachers are effective learners, all of whom have undergraduate degrees and many of whom have graduate degrees. In short, paying attention was not a problem for most teachers when they were students.

Of course, many students *do* have significant problems with attention. In the examples of Jake and Jessica, neither of those students realized that he or she had done anything wrong; Jake and Jessica simply did not realize that paying attention meant, in part, to logically follow the presentation and/or discussion and not to let their thoughts run wild.

> Effective learners learn to mentally "check in" on the class discussion.

In fact, a moment's reflection on what "paying attention" means may be in order here. First of all, no human being can remain focused on one task or issue 100 percent of the time. All learners—children and adults—find that their minds wander off the subject and may fixate momentarily on superfluous thoughts (recall Jake's statement about the go-cart). Given that everyone is off task some percentage of the time, effective learners learn to mentally "check in" on the class discussion. It is this "checking-in" process that is the essence of effective attention skills. As one example, even in everyday conversation, a person often finds that his or her mind has wandered. The person then reorients himself or herself and refocuses on what the conversational partner is saying.

This tuning in—the frequent refocus on the task or conversation—is the essence of attention; it is the skill that is lacking in students with attention problems. This lack of tuning in results in weird or out-of-place comments, or in statements that have nothing to do with the ongoing lesson. This also results in poor performance on seatwork or worksheet types of tasks in the classroom. In short, once Jake's or Jessica's attention wanders outside the classroom, he or she will have a tendency to stay outside the classroom mentally and thus will not accomplish many of the assigned classroom tasks.

> By following the simple procedures outlined here, teachers can assist kids with attention problems to pay attention and to accomplish much more work in the same time frame.

In the 1970s, Daniel Hallahan was the first researcher to recognize this basis for attention problems in students with learning disabilities. He and his coworkers at the University of Virginia developed and provided a way to teach attention skills to kids who did not frequently "check in." By following the simple procedures outlined here, teachers can assist kids with attention problems to pay attention and to accomplish much more work in the same time frame.

## A Personal Example

In addition to a great deal of research that demonstrated the efficacy of self-monitoring (Hallahan & Sapona, 1983; Snider, 1987; Swaggart, 1988), one personal anecdote reflects the importance of this strategy in the lives of kids. I once taught the self-monitoring tactic in a college course in West Virginia, and one of my nontraditional-aged students decided to use it with her 13-year-old daughter who had a learning disability. The daughter had frequently taken two to three hours to complete her homework, and after the mother applied this tactic, the time was cut to approximately one hour each evening. However, that isn't the most telling factor on the effectiveness of this procedure.

After learning self-monitoring, the daughter requested that she be "allowed" to do her self-monitoring in her special education resource class at school also, rather than just during her homework, so that she could more easily finish her work in class. At that point, the mother went to the school to discuss that possibility with the teacher. Of course, the teacher was happy to accommodate the request, but she had never heard of self-monitoring. In fact, she called me at the local college to inquire about this procedure, at which point I called the mother (my student) and subsequently put the whole story together. Of course, not only were the mother and daughter quite excited but I was excited, too, hearing firsthand about someone's success with this tactic. I value strategies that work for kids, their parents, and their teachers, and I have used this story many times in various classes and workshops to motivate teachers to use the self-monitoring strategy. I sincerely believe that every teacher should routinely use this procedure for their kids with attention problems; I have seen it make a qualitative difference in the life of this young girl as well as numerous others.

Using this tactic will allow a teacher to assist students in completing their homework and classwork more quickly and accurately, and the relationship between the teacher and the student will therefore be enhanced.

From the relational discipline perspective, this strategy assists teachers in helping students. Specifically, using this tactic will allow a teacher to assist students in completing their homework and classwork more quickly and accurately, and the relationship between the teacher and the student will therefore be enhanced. Rather than punish students for not completing homework or classwork, teachers can use this tactic to work with students, and, in the process, teach an essential skill that will stay with the students for life.

## What Kids Should Learn This Strategy?

> Students without overt aggression or other overt behavior problems are good candidates for self-monitoring.

The examples of Jake and Jessica, which will seem quite familiar to most teachers, suggest the types of kids for which the self-monitoring strategy is useful. It is intended primarily for kids whose single-biggest problem is attention in class. Students without overt aggression or other overt behavior problems are good candidates for self-monitoring. Most of the early research was done using this strategy with middle school students or students in lower grades, but variations of self-monitoring have been used with students as young as kindergartners and as old as high school juniors and seniors. Since the strategy is not dependent on use of the peer-group influence, there is no restrictive age range when it is likely to be more or less effective.

In fact, the only real restriction is on the type of tasks used with self-monitoring. This procedure should not be used when a student is initially learning new material; rather, it is typically applied during the independent practice phase of learning, when the material has been introduced and practiced with the teacher. In short, the strategy is most effective after the student is doing systematic practice, either on a worksheet or on an appropriate drill and practice computer software program.

## What Is Needed to Teach Kids to Pay Attention?

In order to implement self-monitoring, you will need three things, each of which you may make yourself: a self-monitoring audiotape, a self-monitoring checksheet, and a worksheet of academic problems (i.e., any worksheet you would normally have the kids doing).

### The Self-Monitoring Audiotape

In self-monitoring training to enhance attention, an audiotape is used as the "cue" to make a student attend to the worksheet or other assigned task. This tape may be made using materials in your school or home. Obtain a small tape recorder and a blank audiotape, and sit down at a piano (or with any musical instrument). Begin to record a series of single tones (i.e., using a single note) on the tape. The time between the tones should range between 10 and 90 seconds. Continue until you have approximately 20 minutes of audiotape. You may wish to make several duplicates of this tape so several students can do self-monitoring at once.

### The Self-Monitoring Checksheet

The self-monitoring checksheet is merely a sheet of paper that the student will use to indicate if he or she was paying attention at various points throughout the worksheet activity. This checksheet should have a space for the student's name, the date, and squares or lines in which the student can indicate if he or she was on or off task when the self-monitoring tone sounded. Younger students may benefit from a picture of a "smiley face" to indicate on-task behavior and a "frowning face" to indicate off-task behavior, whereas older students merely need a prompt statement written at the top of the checksheet, such as "Was I paying attention?" Figures 5.1 and 5.2 present two sample checksheets that can be copied and used for different-aged students.

### The Worksheet Task

Students may engage in a variety of subject-matter activities while self-monitoring their own attention behavior. Self-monitoring procedures may be used successfully while students work on arithmetic, handwriting, reading comprehension, and a variety of other academic activities. Also, individualized computer drill and practice activities (as long as they are not time-dependent activities) can be an effective instructional session for implementing a self-monitoring intervention. The content or type of instructional worksheet task really doesn't matter. The only real restriction is that the student should not be in the initial learning stage on the content of the task.

Being more attentive will help the student get homework and classwork done more quickly and therefore give him or her more free time in class.

Name_____ Date_____

**Was I paying attention?**

| Yes | No |
|-----|-----|
|     |     |
|     |     |
|     |     |
|     |     |
|     |     |
|     |     |
|     |     |
|     |     |
|     |     |
|     |     |

**FIGURE 5.1** *Self-Monitoring Checksheet for Older Students*

## Instructional Procedures

Introduce the self-monitoring procedure by telling the student that you want to help him or her to be more attentive. Explain that being more attentive will help the student get homework and classwork done more quickly and therefore give him or her more free time in class. Note that one way to increase attention is to have the student keep track of when he or she is paying attention or not paying attention. Then present the student with the self-monitoring checksheet, the audiotape, and tape recorder, and a worksheet. Explain that the tape is to be played while the student completes the worksheet. Each time the student hears a tone, he or she is to ask himself or herself the question, "Was I paying attention?"

The student will answer that question by marking the checksheet either "yes" or "no" (or "smile" or "frown") and will then return to work on the worksheet. Thus, the tone on the audiotape becomes the cue for the stu-

Name_____ Date_____

## Was I paying attention?

**FIGURE 5.2**  *Self-Monitoring Checksheet for Kindergarten and Younger Students*

dent to refocus on the worksheet task, and the checksheet provides a written record of when the student was paying attention (according to the student). Practice in such refocusing at frequent intervals results in students learning to pay attention and making a habit of that attention skill. In short, you are actually teaching a kid how to pay attention!

Next in the training, describe to the child, in detail, the behaviors that are to be considered paying attention and those that are to be considered not paying attention. For example, if the student is supposed to self-monitor while working on a math assignment, you might explain that paying attention means that the student is seated at his or her desk with pencil in hand, looking at his or her mathematics paper, or consulting with the teacher. Not paying attention during this task might be defined as occurring when the student is talking, laughing, playing with another student, looking out the window, or walking around the room. You should carefully "tailor" your choice of off-task behaviors so that they closely resemble the kinds of off-task behavior of the student for whom the procedure is being used.

> Most students love to "grade the teacher" during this role-play of attention and inattention.

Next, model the use of the self-monitoring checksheet, and have the student identify examples of when you are—and when you are not—paying attention. Most students love to "grade the teacher" during this role-play of attention and inattention. Finally, have the student demonstrate the self-monitoring procedure under your supervision for two to three minutes. During this period, emphasize that each time the student hears a tone, he or she should check the appropriate square on the checksheet and return immediately to work on the worksheet. If you belive the audio tone might disrupt others in the class, have the student use headphones to listen to the tape.

The training procedure should take about 15 to 20 minutes to complete on the first day. As an aid for your training, you may wish to use the script (see Box 5.1) provided by Hallahan, Lloyd, and Stoller (1982) for training the student.

> After two to three days, the student will merely obtain the cueing tape along with a checksheet, and then begin work on the worksheet with no additional instruction.

*Student using self-monitoring*

## BOX 5.1 • *Script for Teacher Introduction of Self-Monitoring*

"Johnny, you know how paying attention to your work has been a problem for you. You've heard teachers tell you, 'Pay attention,' 'Get to work,' 'What are you supposed to be doing?' and things like that. Well, today we're going to start something that will help you help yourself pay attention better.

"First, we need to make sure that you know what paying attention means. This is what I mean by paying attention. (Teacher models immediate and sustained attention to task.) And this is what I mean by not paying attention." (Teacher models inattentive behaviors, such as glancing around and playing with objects.) Now, you tell me if I was paying attention. (Teacher models attentive and inattentive behaviors and requires the student to categorize them.)

"Okay, now let me show you what we're going to do. While you're working, this tape recorder will be turned on. Every once in a while, you'll hear a little sound like this. (Teacher plays tone on tape.) And when you hear that sound, quietly ask yourself, 'Was I paying attention?' If you answer 'yes,' put a check in this box. If you answer 'no,' put a check in this box. Then go right back to work. When you hear the sound again, ask yourself the question, answer it, mark your answer, and go back to work. Now, let me show you how it works. (Teacher models entire procedure.)

"Now, Johnny, I bet you can to this. Tell me what you're going to do every time you hear a tone. Let's try it. I'll start the tape and you work on these papers." (Teacher observes the student's implementation of the entire procedure, praises the child for correctly using the procedure, and gradually withdraws his or her presence.)

On the several days following the initial instruction in self-monitoring, you should briefly review the definition of on- and off-task behavior and the checksheet recording procedures. Make certain that the student has plenty of blank checksheets and is given an appropriate worksheets. After two to three days, using self-monitoring on one or two worksheets each day, the student should grasp the concepts such that, on succeeding days, he or she will merely obtain the cueing tape along with a checksheet, and then begin work on the worksheet with no additional instruction.

### Weaning Procedures

Obviously, it is not in the student's best interests to become dependent on a cassette recorder and a checksheet for monitoring on-task behavior. Therefore, you should plan on weaning the student from the self-monitoring materials after a period of time. Hallahan, Lloyd, and Stoller (1982) have recommended a two-phase weaning procedure. Generally, after a minimum of 10 days using the worksheet, the checksheet, and the audiotape, the student's level of on-task behavior will have increased and you should begin to wean him or her. Thus, after the student has reached a high level of attention using this procedure, you may remove the tape recorder. Hallahan and his coworkers provided a suggested script for this first weaning phase. You might wish to say something like:

> You've been doing really good work on (math, reading, etc.) lately, don't you think? You've been doing so well that I don't think you need to use the tape-recorded tones anymore. Today, whenever you think about it, ask yourself the question, "Was I paying attention?" and then mark your card. Do you have any questions? (Hallahan, Lloyd, & Stoller, 1982)

Point out to the student that he or she is still doing self-monitoring, in that he or she is still using the self-monitoring sheet at this point. Only the tape recorder and audiotape have been removed. Let the student practice self-monitoring in this fashion for three to five days, at a minimum. This will help build a strong "habit" of attention.

After the student has shown his or her ability to self-monitor in this fashion, you may remove the self-monitoring checksheet, as follows:

> You're really doing good work on (math, reading, etc.) without using the tape-recorded tones, don't you think? You've been doing so well that I don't think you need to use the self-monitoring card anymore. I think you can do a really good job without using the tape recorded tones or the self-monitoring card. Today, whenever you think about it, ask yourself the question "Was I paying attention?" If the answer is "Yes" say to yourself "Yes, good job." If the answer is "No," say to yourself, "No, I'd better start paying attention." Do you have any questions? (Hallahan, Lloyd, & Stoller, 1982)

At this point, you have the student doing self-monitoring without any external supports (i.e., no audiotape or checksheet). Consequently, when you or another teacher give a worksheet assignment, the student should be reminded to do his or her self-monitoring. For subsequent assignments, the student should be completing his or her work at a much higher completion level, with a fairly easily implemented procedure that did not take a great deal of your time.

As the preceeding description shows, this is a relatively simple procedure to teach. In fact, the most difficult part of the instruction is understanding when to start the second weaning phase. There are not any hard and fast rules, and the recommendations for a specific number of days are merely guidelines. Of course, at any point during the initial 10 days of training and the weaning phases, if the student's attention skills seem to diminish, you should immediately reinstitute the full procedure (i.e., both audiotape and checksheet) for additional practice. Likewise, if the procedure works for several weeks after the last weaning phase, but the student seems to be slipping back into higher inattention, you may wish to implement the entire procedure again at that point.

In my graduate students' applications of this procedure over the years on the job, I have noted each of these possible results for this procedure. However, I can truthfully state that among my graduate students who implemented this procedure with one student (typically as a class assignment), well over 80 percent have continued to use this procedure for other students. In short, my graduate students have seen the efficacy of this in their own classrooms.

### Does This Really Work?

> This strategy has worked on well over 95 percent of the students in my course projects.

Besides the anecdotal I've shared with you, research on the use of this the self-monitoring procedure is quite positive (Hallahan & Sapona, 1983; Snider, 1987). More pointedly, I have used this procedure myself and had countless undergraduate and graduate students apply this tactic. In my courses, I usually require that my students initially couple this tactic with a time-sampling observation of the student to see if his or her attention skills are actually enhanced. Over the years, this strategy has worked on well over 95 percent of the students in my course projects. The scientific research on the use of self-monitoring indicated that most students who were trained in the procedure could learn it and then be successfully weaned from it (Hallahan & Sapona, 1983). In many cases, this procedure doubles the total time on task for students with attention problems. Further, students showed increased attention abilities for up to 2½ months after the procedure was over (Hallahan & Sapona, 1983). Finally, more recent research indicated that this tactic is very effective even with students with attention deficit hyperactive disorders who were also taking prescribed drugs to enhance their attention (Mathes & Bender, 1996). Clearly, this is a procedure that every teacher should have at his or her fingertips for those inattentive kids in the classroom.

> Students showed increased attention abilities for up to 2½ months after the procedure was over

## *Adaptations of Self-Monitoring for Other Problem Behaviors*

As discussed to this point, the self-monitoring procedure serves the purpose of enhancing attention and work completion. However, after the early research on using self-monitoring to improve attention skills, many researchers began to apply these same procedures to enhance behavior in other areas, as well.

> Self-monitoring for class preparedness has been shown to be a highly effective variation on the application of self-monitoring.

For example, every teacher, at one time or another, has been frustrated when an otherwise talented child simply forgets his books or other materials constantly. Self-monitoring for class preparedness has been shown to be a highly effective variation on the application of self-monitoring. For that procedure, a tape recorder and audiotape are not needed. Rather, you may create an activity in which students indicate their class preparedness at the first of the period. The checklist in Figure 5.3 can be adjusted for use with inattentive and chronically unprepared students at the beginning of each period. If the indicators in Figure 5.3 do not capture the specific behavior or preparedness issues that need to be addressed for a particular child, you can easily adapt the checksheet by adding another column or different labels.

It is also possible to have students self-monitor almost any type of behavior, from academic performance to specific problem behaviors. For example, students may be trained to check off each time they blurt out an answer without raising their hand, each time they use obscene language, or each time they call another student a name. In many cases, merely having students self-monitor their own negative behaviors can lead to a decrease in those behaviors. Again, this strategy can prepare you to deal with a variety of behavior problems in the class without taking a great deal of your time.

**Weekly Record of Class Preparedness**

| | Monday | Tuesday | Wednesday | Thursday | Friday |
|---|---|---|---|---|---|
| Has pencil on desk and ready | | | | | |
| Has paper for note taking | | | | | |
| Has books ready for study | | | | | |
| Has completed all homework | | | | | |
| Is in the seat at the bell | | | | | |
| Is quiet when class begins | | | | | |

**FIGURE 5.3**   *Checksheet for Class Preparedness*

## Group Contingencies

In a group contingency intervention, the group is rewarded and/or punished based on the behaviors of one or more group members.

Another type of tactic for kids with attention problems involves the use of the peer group as a support for attention (Salend, Whittaker, & Reeder, 1992). Students like Jake and Jessica, described earlier, are quite common in most classrooms, and using a group-oriented reward system for supporting attention skills can elicit the input from the peer group in a positive fashion (Jenson & Reavis, 1999; Salend, Whittaker, & Reeder, 1992).

In a group contingency intervention, the group is rewarded and/or punished based on the behaviors of one or more group members (Salend, Whittaker, & Reeder, 1992). Thus, from the relational disciplinary perspective, this tactic involves harnessing the power of the peer group during or after the peer influence period (discussed in Chapter 2). Students generally can find ways to improve their behavior—even ingrained and habitual behavior such as attention—when the power and influence of the peer group is brought to bear.

> The group contingency tactic can build successful interpersonal relationships.

Also, if this strategy works, the group begins to develop a group identity, which can be a powerful relationship builder for many kids. Specifically, students with learning disabilities and/or attention deficit disorders often demonstrate some difficulty making and fostering interpersonal relationships; using the group contingency tactic can build more successful interpersonal relationships for many of these students. It is always a wonderful result when any disciplinary strategy can foster appropriate relationships for kids, and this is a tactic that can profoundly influence kids toward positive relationships with others.

> In the individual-all group contingency, the behavior of one person dramatically impacts everyone, and the peer pressure is likely to be somewhat stronger for that person to improve his or her behavior.

Jenson and Reavis (1999) identified several types of group contingency. In the *individual-all group contingency* situation, the behavior of one individual determines the reward for the entire group. In the *group-all group contingency*, the specific target behaviors of every member of the group are recorded, and the reward is based on the total group's behavior. The teacher must make a choice as to which type of contingency he or she wishes to use. In the individual-all group contingency, the behavior of one person dramatically impacts everyone, and the peer pressure is likely to be somewhat stronger for that person to improve his or her behavior. The advantage for the group-all group contingency strategy is that the entire group will be monitoring and seeking improvement in the behavior of every member of the group, and the strategy is likely to result in improved classroom behavior overall (Salend, Whittaker, & Reeder, 1992).

*Group contingencies work!*

## What Kids Should Learn This Strategy?

> Group contingencies will work for many kids with a wide array of behavioral problems.

Unlike the self-monitoring discussed previously, this strategy is dependent on the influence of the peer group, and even though teachers in lower grades may try this tactic (it will often work even in the lower grades), the strategy will probably be more effective for kids in fourth grade and higher. For example, Salend, Whittaker, and Reeder (1992) demonstrated the efficacy of this tactic for students between 11 and 15 years of age. Further, although this strategy is particularly effective for kids with attention problems (thus the placement of this tactic in this chapter), the strategy also quite helpful for kids who may be aggressive or even violent. Again, the power of the influence of peers is quite profound, and therefore this strategy will work for many kids with a wide array of behavioral problems.

Finally, by using the group contingency strategy, you will be establishing groups throughout the class, as described next, as well as including kids with all types of behavior problems to help reduce those problems. The only caveat to bear in mind is the possibility that you may lose control of the strategy. For example, if a aggressive or violent student finds himself or herself being asked to "please work more quietly" by a classmate, the aggressive student may lose it; anger could flair or verbal or physical aggression toward the other student may result. Obviously, you will have to control this tactic very carefully, and, in fact, may decide not to apply it for certain students.

## Implementing a Group Contingency

A number of models of group contingency interventions are available in the literature (Jenson & Reavis, 1999; Salend, Whittaker, & Reeder, 1992), and there are several common elements for your consideration. These include establishing comparable groups, specifying a target behavior for each student or group member, stating ground rules for polite requests, establishing an easily understood contingency, and establishing a reward system. These things must be attended to when using this tactic in order to assure success.

> The idea is to establish groups of kids with roughly comparable behavior who can work together to suitably and politely remind each other of appropriate behavior.

As an example, imagine the following group contingency intervention to address the frequent inattentive behavior of 3 specific students in your class of 21 kids. You would first establish three groups of 7 kids each such that each of the various inattentive kids is in a different group. You should also take care to place kids who are aggressive or who overtly misbehave in various groups. The idea is to establish groups of kids with roughly comparable behavior who can work together to suitably and politely remind each other of appropriate behavior. Some teachers use the option of letting kids choose various group members, and then "trust to luck" that the groups will be relatively equal. If this is attempted and the groups do not seem equal, the judicious and considered movement of several kids can usually result in comparable groups.

After groups are established, you should carefully select a specific behavior for each group member in which you would like to see improvement (Jenson & Reavis, 1999). The behavior for each student must be clearly defined and easily observable. Each target behavior should also be discussed with the student in terms of making improvement a personal goal of the student. Also, each student should understand that his or her target behavior may be different from that of other group members.

It is not uncommon to find kids today who do not know how to make a polite request.

Once the behaviors are specified, establish some "supportive" ground rules about the types of things that kids should say to each other to remind them of appropriate attention behaviors. Because of the inappropriate conversation models often promoted by movies, television, records, and other mass media, it is not uncommon to find kids today who do not know how to make a polite request. Thus, the skill of politely requesting should be directly taught to the kids as you implement this tactic. Of course, you probably model polite requesting in your class daily, and such modeling will help, but still the manner of making these polite requests should be discussed and/or taught to the kids.

Some suggested forms for particular requests may assist your students in understanding the types of things to say. (You might want to copy these examples on a wall chart and post it in your classroom.) These may include the following:

"Alphonzo, please remember to do your work quickly."

"Luis, please remember that this is worktime, and our group wants to win the prize for today of extra recess time."

"Sally, could you please work more quietly so that I can finish my work on time?"

You should rehearse the class in statements like these. You might also consider putting these examples and other appropriate prototypes on a poster on the wall. Further, you should remind the class to use an appropriate tone of voice when making their polite requests. Finally, give the kids a guideline on what to do if their polite request to a group member results in making that group member angry. Kids should be told to ignore any angry remarks made by a group member in response to a polite request for better behavior. At that point, you will need to step in and deal directly with the angry student.

In establishing the specific group-all group contingency, you should consider several things, including the overall clarity of the group requirement and graduated rewards for various groups. Here is an example:

The group with the best behavior may earn 10 minutes of extra physical education time this afternoon if I don't have to deal with more that two overt behavior problems from that group during the day. The next group may earn up to 5 minutes of extra PE time. The third group doesn't earn any extra time.

In using this contingency, the specific inattentive behavior of the student with attention problems should be discussed with that student, and perhaps with the group as a whole. For example, you decide to ask Jake for permission to discuss with the group his lack of attention. You then point out to the group that Jake wants the group's assistance in staying on task so that he can help the group earn the reward time. Therefore, the group members should help Jake through gentle reminders during the classwork assignments. Ask various group members to demonstrate the types of off-task behavior that they should watch for. Then role-play with those students how they might remind Jake to return to his work in order to help the group earn the reward.

Note in the preceding example that this contingency allows for rewards to be offered to several groups. This variation will enhance the effectiveness of the overall tactic. In short, there is no reason for group members to "give up" simply because one student in that group demonstrated inappropriate behavior.

The reward system used in group contingencies may involve any type of rewards for which the students will work. Extra PE time, recess time, or work time on a fun project are considered appropriate motivators. Many teachers have found that students can be motivated by the option of extra time on the computer in the classroom. For kids with attention problems, computer-assisted instruction often offers not only a motivational workplace but also a work medium that can hold their attention if appropriate software has been selected.

## Conclusion

In relational discipline, improved behavior and the relationship between the teacher and the student are both critical. The tactics discussed in this chapter result in improving both the classroom behaviors as well as the all-important relationship. Further, Salend, Whittaker, and Reeder (1992) even demonstrated a method for combining self-monitoring and group contingencies, and the adventurous teacher may wish to investigate that procedure, using their article from the reference list. Still, the tactics of self-monitoring and group contingencies offer the teacher a series of options to assist students with attention behaviors, and every teacher should employ some variation of these options when appropriate in his or her classroom.

## References

Bender, W. N. (1997). *Understanding ADHD: A practical guide for teachers and parents*. Columbus, OH: Merrill.

Hallahan, D. P., Lloyd, J. W., & Stoller, L. (1982). *Improving attention with self-monitoring: A manual for teachers*. Charlottesville, VA: Curry School of Education, University of Virginia.

Hallahan, D. P., & Sapona, R. (1983). Self-monitoring of attention with learning disabled children: Past research and current issues. *Journal of Learning Disabilities, 16*, 616–620.

Jenson, W. R., & Reavis, H. K. (1999). Using group contingencies to improve academic achievement. *Best Practices, 1*, 77–84.

Mathes, M. O., & Bender, W. N. (1996). Effects of self-monitoring on children with attention deficit disorders who are receiving medical interventions: Implications for inclusive instruction. *Remedial and Special Education, 18*, 121–128.

Salend, S. J., Whittaker, C. R., & Reeder, E. (1992). Group evaluation: A collaborative peer-mediated behavior management system. *Exceptional Children, 59*, 203–209.

Snider, V. (1987). Use of self-monitoring of attention with LD students: Research and application. *Learning Disability Quarterly, 10*, 139–151.

Swaggart, B. L. (1988). Implementing a cognitive behavior management program. *Intervention in School and Clinic, 33* (4), 235–238.

## Chapter 6

# Putting It All Together

## A Relational Discipline Classroom

One frustration of many in education is the "cookbook" approach applied to various disciplinary programs, without an underlying insight into what really results in effective discipline in a classroom. Numerous discipline books offer an array of effective tactics, but in many approaches, there seems to be no underlying construct that ties the various tactics together. This often leaves professional educators unsatisfied. Many feel that some overriding goal or set of values is necessary to guide them in selection of specific tactics, and unfortunately, many disciplinary systems simply do not provide that underlying construct.

> Punishments and rewards may impact minor behaviors, but it is relationships that result in a student internalizing a disciplinary standard for appropriate behavior over the long term.

As a primary focus, the relational discipline approach stipulates that relationships are the basis for effective discipline. Punishments and rewards may impact minor behaviors, but it is relationships that result in a student internalizing a disciplinary standard for appropriate behavior over the long term. From this relational discipline perspective, all the strategies and tactics discussed in previous chapters, as well as many other specific tactics (indeed, there are numerous effective strategies and tactics that have not even been mentioned in this book!), must be evaluated on several sim-

*Teaching is fun!*

ple questions. One purpose of this chapter is to provide insight into these questions, and thereby address how a teacher may approach a certain disciplinary situation, based on the solid underlying framework of relational discipline.

The second purpose of this chapter is to consider discipline from the perspective of the entire classroom. In some cases, a classwide disciplinary tactic may be needed in order to establish or reestablish high disciplinary expectations. One tactic, the Let's Make a Deal strategy, is suggested later in the chapter for such a situation.

Next, as I have noted numerous times, discipline is not exclusively a one-to-one relationship. From the broader social perspective, relationships are multifaceted and multidimensional, and disciplinary approaches must likewise be broadly based and involve consideration of all the possible relationships within the class setting (and/or other settings in which a child functions). As stated in Chapter 1, discipline strategies must, at certain ages, involve the peer group and all class members in order to be effective. During the peer intervention period—as the single-best example—application of simple rewards and punishments are not likely to be effective, unless the teacher has structured these to impact the peers overall.

Thus, the third purpose of this chapter is to focus on the larger issue of how a class as a whole responds to the teacher's approach to discipline. This focus, often referred to as *classroom climate* (Hansen & Childs, 1998; Sterling, 1998), comprises the final section of this chapter. It will offer some suggestions on assessment of classroom climate and options to change the overall experiential sense of the classroom. Upon consideration, it is apparent that the classroom is the primary context for the relationships between students, their peers, and their teachers. Thus, the climate established in a relational discipline classroom is critical.

This chapter is designed to pull together the concept of relational discipline so that teachers can teach in a classroom founded on such an approach. In order to accomplish this, we must first consider the assessment and planning context for disciplinary problems.

## A Paradigm Shift: Strength-Based Assessment

Michael Epstein of the University of Nebraska in Lincoln has recognized a weakness in the current thinking about discipline for students with significant behavior problems (i.e., discipline for in-your-face kids) (Epstein, 1998, 1999; Rudolph & Epstein, 2000). This weakness involves the fact that traditional behavior management assessments and planning options are rooted in deficits rather than strengths. In his work, Epstein has begun to shift from the behavior management paradigm for these in-your-face students (Epstein, 2000).

The typical assessment and remediation planning for most students with behavior problems would involve an intellectual, behavioral, and academic assessment, and would basically result in a plethora of negative findings. Epstein, however, has recommended that instead of conducting such a negative assessment, one identifies the strengths that operate for the benefit of a student with severe behavioral problems. According to Epstein (2000), such a strength-based assessment may involve a chat with a child and/or a discussion with the child's parents on the overall contextual environment for the child. The typical questions from a strength-based assessment may include:

What are the best things about you?
Who are your closest friends?
What is your neighborhood like?
How do you picture yourself five years from now?

These questions may be easily adapted to be used in an interview with a parent about a child and his or her behavior. With such an informal assessment option, the discussion may be quite open, and every effort should be made to foster a comfortable atmosphere during these discussions. When such an atmosphere can be created, surprising findings of potential strengths may be unearthed, which go far beyond the litany of deficits that result from traditional assessment practices. A brief comparison of the "findings" from a traditional assessment and a strength-based assessment is presented in Box 6.1 (see Epstein [2000] for a similar comparison).

Note that the findings from the traditional assessment and planning process merely present a list of deficit areas, and offer no real solutions. Teachers and parents are often frustrated when presented with such a catalogue of negative findings. In fact, when presented with findings similar to these, veteran teachers often feel as if they could have written the evaluation based merely on their observations. Youngsters with serious behavior problems are often quite similar in their areas of deficit, and behavioral deficits often lead to or occur with academic deficits. Thus, the traditional assessment rarely presents "big news" findings that offer positive intervention possibilities (Epstein, 2000). Further, there is very little in traditional assessment practices that even hints at the relationships which a student may have, and from the relational discipline perspective, those relationships are critical.

In contrast, a strength-based assessment poses a variety of questions not typically asked in traditional assessments, and many of those questions

**BOX 6.1 • *Traditional Assessment and Strength-Based Assessment***

For a given fifth-grade student with significant behavioral problems, a traditional assessment versus a strength-based assessment might look like this. Note how the strength-based assessment offers possible connections with the student, whereas the traditional assessment is merely a catalogue of problems, offering no potential solutions.

### *Conclusions from a Traditional Assessment*
- Has lower than average IQ (FSIQ = 87)
- Sent to in-school suspension five times in three months
- Had two fights with students
- Has poor academic skills in reading and all reading-dependent subject areas
- Has received special education services for three years
- Manifests aggression and other externalizing disorders

### *Conclusions from a Strength-Based Assessment*
- Plays basketball with a minister in the community several afternoons each week
- Functions on grade level in math
- Is "sportsmanlike" on the basketball court
- Has mother who is actively involved and comes to all IEP meetings

*Teachers enjoy strength-based assessment.*

focus on relationships that are meaningful for the child. Epstein (1998, 2000) maintains that, unlike traditional assessment, strength-based assessment frequently offers something positive for parents and teachers to discuss relative to a child. This factor alone can enhance the relationship between the parents and the teacher, and well as between the teacher and the child.

Because of the focus on relationships as one potential strength for children with behavioral problems, a classroom founded on relational discipline must include a number of informal assessments that focus on strengths of the child with problems. Several of these are offered later in this chapter. However, the debt to Michael Epstein cannot be overemphasized; the strength-based assessment construct that he developed truly represents a critical paradigm shift in assessment and intervention planning for troubled youngsters.

## A Classwide Negotiation: Let's Make a Deal!

One way to challenge any disciplinary system is to consider the numerous problems when an entire classroom is out of control. I was recently challenged to do a workshop on discipline in the following context: An inner-city school was about to be taken over by the courts because of low school-wide performance. (How many times have educators recently heard of this scenario in the national education press!) This school had serious disciplinary problems, had replaced several teachers for the special education classrooms (classes that included mostly kids with behavioral disorders), and had invited me to do a workshop for the remaining teachers. In one extreme case, a new, first-year teacher had just been hired to get control of one of the classes from which a veteran teacher had recently retired. To make matters more challenging, it was only three months prior to the end of the school year! Although I've faced a number of serious situations in my career working to strengthen discipline in schools around the nation, I quickly realized that this was going to be one of my most challenging workshops. However, upon reflection, I felt somewhat guilty for that self-pity. Although I had to conceptualize a few tactics for this situation, my job was finished in a one-day workshop, whereas the teachers with whom I was working had to face those middle school adolescents every single day!

In a situation like this, a new teacher or perhaps a newly transferred teacher will need to establish or reestablish himself or herself as having a legitimate role in the class. Thus, some negotiation of power with the students is in order. I devised such a negotiation tactic: Let's Make a Deal! The strategy involves a 10-step process for the teacher to undertake with the students after he or she has spent one or two days in the classroom. It involves eliciting from the students in class how they see the role and responsibilities of each other and of the teacher. If a teacher in this situation can construct an activity that encourages the students to empower that teacher in some fashion, then the teacher will be leagues ahead in reestablishing discipline in a situation in which previously there was none (see Box 6.2).

## BOX 6.2 • *The Purpose of the Let's Make a Deal Tactic*

The purpose of the Let's Make a Deal tactic is to develop with the class a class portrait or representation of the roles and responsibilities of various class members. This will present the teacher with a number of unique opportunities:

1. The teacher will have the opportunity to assist in defining for various class members a more positive role for himself or herself, based on the strengths and perceptions of class members.
2. The teacher will have the opportunity to have the class help define his or her role, and thus empower the teacher for various tasks in the classroom.
3. The teacher will have the opportunity to negotiate a power-sharing responsibility for one or more power students in the class, which gives those students a positive role responsibility, perhaps for the first time, in the class.

### Ten Steps in Let's Make a Deal

**1.** *Identify the Power Kid.* As a first step, you need to identify the single-most influential student in the class. This student (or students), known as the Power Kid, will help determine the relationships between you and all the students in the class. Once the Power Kid has been identified, you must arrange a negotiation of power with that student, and, through him or her, the power struggle with the remaining members of the class will fall into place.

**2.** *Seek a self-description.* Tell the class that you want to draw a picture of the friendships and roles of each class member. Request that one child (not the Power Kid) go to the board and give himself or herself a descriptive name and/or several descriptive indicators of who he/she is and what role he or she plays in the classroom. For example, Franklin might name himself as the class clown: "I make folks laugh!" or "I'm the class entertainer." Alternatively, Maria may describe herself by a role she plays in class: "I'm a peacemaker" or "I'm the best reader." You should elicit positive descriptions and ignore all negative descriptions. Have the student write several positive statements near his or her name and then draw a circle on the board around his or her chosen name and the description. You then review the descriptions and compliment the student on his or her positive role in the class.

**3.** *Discuss the descriptions.* Discuss the description with the class and elicit the students' views of these descriptions for the student at the chalkboard. Again, ignore all negative comments and seek only positive comments; if possible, add to the descriptive statements any positive comments the class might make about the student's role. You may also wish to elicit certain comments on particular roles common in groups of students (e.g., class leader, class clown, peacemaker, committee leader, the judge, class cop, big man, etc.). Use the assistance of many students, particularly those who have identified roles for themselves along these lines.

**4.** *Repeat the process with one or two more youngsters.* Have several more students describe themselves and their roles in the class in positive terms. Instruct the second and third students to locate themselves either near or away from the first student so that you can get a picture of the friendships within the class. Also, be certain that these first few students do not use the center of the board. Again, emphasize the positive aspects of the descriptions, and compliment the kids on their importance in the class.

**5.** *Select the Power Kid.* At this point, you request that the Power Kid describe himself or herself. Once the Power Kid sees you compliment the previous students, chances are good that he or she will want to participate. Be obvious in noting the positive reactions of the class, and, based on that anticipated reaction, suggest that the Power Kid place himself or herself in the center of the board. Compliment him or her as a class leader, and inquire about what role responsibilities leadership entails. If possible, elicit a statement from this student about his or her influence in the class, or possibly his or her power.

**6.** *Negotiate power.* When the Power Kid has finished, mention that power and influence involve some responsibilities as well as some authority. Ask the class what power the class wishes to give to this student. For example, perhaps the Power Kid should have a "veto of assignment" power. This means that he or she can veto one assignment during any given week—any worksheet or homework (though not a test) that you might assign. This will mean that you must always have an alternative assignment in your desk, but it can also mean that you have earned some cooperation from the most influential student in the class. If the class requests another choice option or that another student share in the class power, you should consider that as an option to offer the Power Kid.

**7.** *Finish with the other participating students.* Once you have negotiated with the Power Kid, you then undertake this tactic with other participating students in the class. In small classes (of 10 or less), you should do this with everyone in the class. In large classes, you will need to invite six or eight strategically selected students to participate in the Let's Make a Deal tactic, while the others conduct an assignment outside of class.

**8.** *Develop an "Influence Portrait."* When all participating students are on the chalkboard, draw lines and/or arrows to identify friendships between those who are friendly with each other. Closer relationships should be depicted in close proximity on the board, and you may need to "move" students after some class discussion. Explain to the students that this portrait represents the friendships and levels of influence in the class, and encourage them to suggest any additional modifications in the portrait as necessary.

**9.** *Place yourself.* As a culmination for this activity, ask the class, "Is anyone missing?" With this question, you can find out if they think to include you. If you need to prompt them, ask them if you, as the teacher, have any positive role or responsibilities for what goes on. Elicit descriptions such as "Teaching us something important," "Making meaningful assignments,"

"Making school fun," "Caring for the students," and so on. You might wish to ask the class if you have a right to make class or homework assignments or to assign role-plays or computer work? If the class says no, you may tell them that you have to sometimes, and inquire about making such assignments only two or three times a week. In this manner, you may be able to negotiate your way into some influence in this difficult classroom situation where previously you had none. If you can get the class to acknowledge your role as teacher, you have empowered yourself in a relational disciplinary sense. More accurately, the class has empowered you do the things that you could not do in a class with no established disciplinary expectations.

**10.** *Write up the deal!* Tell the class that no deal is a deal unless it is in writing and everyone signs it. List the roles of the class leaders (or all class members), including their expected contributions, and the veto (or other) powers that you have agreed to share. Also list your role and responsibilities as the teacher. Attach a copy of the class portrait from the chalkboard, and then pass that document out to each member of the class. You may also wish to post a copy for later use. Have everyone sign a copy, and then use that as a statement of what you, the teacher, should do in the class.

## When to Use Let's Make a Deal

When a teacher is considering sharing power with the students, he or she is merely acknowledging the reality of classrooms today—effective teachers negotiate with students all the time. As indicated in the preceeding example, this tactic can be very useful in extreme situations where a class is out of control.

However, you might also wish to consider this as an interesting social skill activity in many classes that are not out of control. As teachers, we may be somewhat surprised by the views that some students have of us. It is often interesting to inquire of students what role they see for the teacher in schools today.

As a researcher, I must point out that there is no supportive research with this particular tactic. However, to my knowledge, there are no guidelines anywhere for reestablishing discipline when a class is "out of control." You may find that this emphasis on negotiated relationships and responsibilities is the most effective use of your time, should you ever find yourself in this type of rather extreme disciplinary situation. Box 6.3 presents the steps of Let's Make a Deal, in a nutshell form.

**BOX 6.3 •** *Steps in the Let's Make a Deal Tactic*

1. Identify the Power Kid. Use two or three other students initially and avoid using the Power Kid first.
2. Seek a self-description. Have another student select a descriptive name/ role description for himself or herself, and write three to five positive indicators of that role on the chalkboard, which represents the student's role in the class (e.g., class clown, peacemaker, the judge, etc.).
3. Discuss the descriptions with the class. Ascertain their accuracy and add any additional positive descriptions.
4. Repeat with the other students. Have a second then a third student do the same process. They should locate themselves (on the chalkboard) close to their friends and far away from those they know less well.
5. Select the Power Kid. Discuss his or her roles and responsibilities with the students and with the class. In a complimentary fashion, acknowledge the power and influence he or she has in the class.
6. Negotiate power. Negotiate with the Power Kid and the class a sharing of power with the Power Kid(s), perhaps a once-a-week "assignment veto."
7. Finish with the other students. Every child in the class should be included, if possible. If not, include every influential child.
8. Draw an "Influence Portrait." Draw a picture of the class relationships based on the information on the chalkboard, and discuss the relationships and the influence between students as presented in the drawing.
9. Place yourself. Ask the class if you have a role in the class. Ask what types of things a teacher is expected to do in a school class, and be prepared to negotiate some of those roles (e.g., homework assignments are OK but not on weekends, or perhaps only three days a week).
10. Write up and sign the deal. Include the class portrait, the descriptions of various roles, and any shared power arrangements in the class.

## Guiding Questions in Relational Discipline

### The Fundamentals of Relational Discipline

With the strength-based paradigm shift in mind, along with a strategy that allows a teacher to negotiate power with an entire class, we can now focus on some basics that will assist in implementation of relational discipline for the class as a whole. You may recall from Chapter 1 that discipline was based on three things: a student's need for attention, relationships with others, and a developmental progression to self-discipline. As described earlier, the student's attention tank must be filled when he or she wishes, and in the manner that he or she wishes, in order to foster development of effective nurturing relationships and the eventual internalization of appropriate disciplinary standards. Thus, the following three underlying questions can effectively guide teachers toward particular strategies for particular students:

1. What and who can fill this child's need for attention right now?
2. What can I do to foster this child's relationship with me and with others in the class?
3. What can I do to facilitate this child's internal desire to behave more appropriately in the future?

> The more prepared one is in advance for disciplinary disruptions, the more effective one is as a disciplinarian.

With these questions in mind, the teacher will progress through as logical series of steps when confronted with a disciplinary problem. Veteran teachers will realize that they can do this reflective thought in advance for many of their students, and the more prepared one is in advance for disciplinary disruptions, the more effective one is as a disciplinarian.

## Guiding Questions

The underlying principles of relational discipline, then, provide guidance on how to handle disciplinary problems as they occur in the classroom. Issues include: What type of behavior is demonstrated, and how does that get attention for the student in a way that is pleasing to the student? Is the behavior explosive, consistent, or infrequent? How are the student's attention needs currently being met by others in the classroom? How can the teacher build a relationship with this student that fosters long-term internalization of discipline?

In order to assist teachers in implementing relational discipline thinking, Box 6.4 presents a series of questions that teachers may use when considering a particular student's attention tank needs within the classroom. This checklist is intended merely as a reminder of the types of attention needs and the potential strategies that may address those needs. Reflective thought on these questions, in advance of disruptive behaviors in the classroom, is one hallmark of an effective relational discipline classroom.

**BOX 6.4 • *Analysis of Attention Needs***

1. What type of behavior does this child usually demonstrate? Is it typical behavior as described in one of these chapters (e.g., aggressive/noncompliant, attention seeking, etc.)? _____

   _____

2. Describe the child's most recent behavioral outburst. Was it typical of him or her? Was it in response to another student?

   _____

   _____

3. Does the student behave in this fashion consistently? Is the behavior explosive? Will I need to use diffusion tactics?

   _____

   _____

4. How did the peers in the class respond to this child's misbehavior? Positively or negatively? _____

   _____

   _____

5. What type of attention need was being filled for this child and by what mechanism (e.g., Was other students' laughter a reward for misbehavior? Did other students react negatively?)?

   _____

   _____

6. How can I, as the teacher, value the student's attention need and redirect it in a more positive fashion? _____

   _____

   _____

7. Was the child happy with the response from the class (either positive or negative)?_____

   _____

8. Have particular disciplinary techniques failed with this child?

   _____

   _____

   _____

**BOX 6.4** **Continued**

9. Are there examples from other teachers of disciplinary ideas that worked or did not work for this child? Can those experiences provide some guidance?_____

_____

_____

10. From what I can tell, this student's attention needs are currently fulfilled by:

_____

_____

11. Is a particular tactic suggested by these attention needs (e.g., would a responsibility strategy, mentorship, etc.)?

_____

_____

12. This student has a number of strengths and special areas of knowledge that can be built upon. They are:

_____

_____

> Effective teachers constantly and consistently reflect not only on what tactics may work but also on their own internal reactions to, and relationship with, the offending child and his or her behavior.

As the questions in Box 6.4 indicate, the teacher's immediate concern is reflection on the specific types of behavior that the child demonstrates. The first several questions assist in determining the type and frequency of behavior (e.g., explosive behavior, his or her most recent outburst, etc.). Next, some consideration is given to the responses of the class members to the behavior (e.g., Was the response positive or negative? Did the disruptive student enjoy his or her interactions with the class?). Next, the teacher should consider disciplinary tactics that may not have worked for that child previously, using input from the teacher's own experience as well as the experience of other teachers. Note that the teacher's responses to several questions on this form may lead directly to particular interventions (e.g., diffusion tactics, mentoring, etc.). Finally, note that several questions in this checklist are framed around the teacher's own reactions to the child and the offending behavior (e.g., questions 6 and 12). Effective teachers constantly and consistently reflect not only on what tactics may work but also on their own internal reactions to, and relationship with, the offending child and his or her behavior.

After consideration of the attention needs of the child, some consideration must be given to an informal strength-based assessment that focuses on fostering relationships. Box 6.5 presents a series of guiding questions to assist in this reflection.

> Only after building an effective and enjoyable relationship with the kid can the teascher hope to discipline the child effectively over the long term.

The questions in Box 6.5 reflect consideration of the student's attitudes toward himself or herself and others. Indications of respect for the teacher and peers will often provide guidance on how to respond to disciplinary problems within the classroom. Again, the teacher must specifically reflect on building an effective and enjoyable relationship with the kid in question. Only then can the teacher hope to discipline a child effectively over the long term. Also, this reflective checklist again identifies several particular strategies that may be prompted by the analysis of the child's social experience in the classroom. Tactics such as Shine My Light, mentoring, and classroom structuring for clingy or insecure kids may result from consideration of a child's needs in relation to his or her peer relationships and/or the relationship with the teacher.

> The ultimate goal of any relational discipline plan must be to help the student internalize appropriate behavioral standards for himself or herself.

Finally, Box 6.6 presents several questions that may guide you in consideration of assisting the child to internalize an appropriate disciplinary standard. The ultimate goal of any relational discipline plan must be to help the student internalize appropriate behavioral standards for himself or herself. In short, students must experience the sense that their attention needs will be meet through behaviors that are desirable in the class, and not through negative behaviors. Students will then begin to behave in a more

**BOX 6.5 • *Fostering Positive Relationships***

1. What can I do to foster a positive relationship between this student and me as well as between this student and others in the class?

   _____

   _____

2. Does this child currently respect me as his or her teacher?_____

   _____

3. Does this child currently respect his or her peers?_____

   _____

4. Does this child currently respect himself or herself? _____

   _____

5. Is this child secure with his or her social position in the classroom (e.g., Is the child clingy? Is a relaxation approach appropriate?)

   _____

   _____

6. Should this child be confronted with the thoughts/analysis of his or her peers concerning the behavioral outburst? _____

   _____

7. As a teacher, I feel that I can best establish rapport with this child by (e.g., time together, after-school activity, caring statements, using him or her as a tutor/helper, etc.):_____

   _____

8. This student's needs are so great that another adult should be found to provide a mentorship relationship in which the student feels valued. I can begin that process by: _____

   _____

9. Should I encourage a student report (or Shine My Light) time that focuses on this student's special knowledge? How does that fit into a subject area and when?_____

   _____

   _____

10. Can I establish a method for this child to earn rewards for other kids in the class through more appropriate behavior?

    _____

    _____

appropriate fashion, and will work toward continued improved behavior, as long as their needs are being met. The simple method for accomplishing this is open discussions with the child about his or her behavior, in the context of a developing relationship with the teacher.

Box 6.6 presents several ideas about how a teacher may foster that relationship, including using the relationships that the child has already developed with other adults. Perhaps two adults (e.g., the teacher and an adult who has a positive relationship previously established with the child) could meet with the child together.

**BOX 6.6** • *Internalizing Discipline*

1. What can I do to facilitate this child's internal desire to behave more appropriately in the future? _____

   _____

2. Based on my analysis of this child's attention needs, I can begin to fill his or her attention needs by:

   _____

   _____

3. Can I develop routinely scheduled opportunities for this student to participate meaningfully in class, which will result in the student having a privilege or responsibility that others don't have? _____

   _____

   _____

4. What peers can I involve in reinforcing appropriate behavior for this student (e.g., study buddies)? Is it possible to pair this student who has a student with more appropriate behaviors? _____

   _____

   _____

5. What other adult is important to this child, and can I request that that adult speak with this child about improvements in behavior? Can I use the relationship between that adult and the child to foster an improved relationship between myself and the child?_____

   _____

   _____

### Additional Options for Fostering Positive Relationships

One interesting point needs to made here about the structure of U.S. schools. You may recall from discussions in Chapter 1 how the development of the departmentalized school curriculum essentially breaks down the relationships between students and teachers at the secondary level. Unfortunately, other aspects of current school structures also break down these relationships at the lower grade levels—specifically, the standard practice of changing teachers at the end of each school year.

> It is unfortunate that the current structure of schools breaks the student/ teacher relationship at the end of the school year by moving the student with behavior problems into another class.

The development of a positive relationship between any teacher and a student with behavioral problems often takes quite a while. In some cases, it may take half the school year or more. If such a positive relationship is finally established between a teacher and a problem student, it is an unfortunate fact that the current structure of schools breaks that relationship at the end of the school year, by moving the student with the behavior problems into another class. The positive relationship between the child and a new teacher must then be established all over again. This can be very destructive for children, since such positive relationships are rare for problem kids anyway and are often quite difficult to establish. In fact, for most kids with behavior problems, if a positive relationship is established with one teacher, it is not likely that many other positive relationships will be established with other teachers, simply because the child may feel somewhat "abandoned" at the end of the year. He or she may then begin the next year with even more overt behavioral problems. Again, the very structure and organization of schools tends to hurt kids and lead to the breakdown of the critical pupil/teacher relationship.

> Teachers can follow the children across grade levels and thus maintain the positive structured relationship with each member of the class.

Many educators nationwide have noted this problem and have begun to respond through the option of looping. Looping means that the teacher essentially follows the children across grade levels—typically teaching the same group of 20 to 25 kids for up to three years—and thus maintains the positive structured relationship with each member of the class. The only real limitation on the practice is the certification limitations of the teacher. In most states, the elementary teaching certificate allows teachers to teach any grade from kindergarten through grade 6 or 7. In theory, then, a teacher could teach the same children for seven years. In practice, though, looping generally involves the teacher working with the same class for a period of two or three years.

Although looping is currently practiced in only a limited number of schools, the practice is receiving national attention, and many more schools and school districts are considering this option. Looping allows for the meaningful establishment of longer-term relationships, and thus this practice can foster much improved behavior on the part of children with problems. Only future research will tell if such promises are realized.

> You might try to transfer the positive relationship between last year's teacher and the child to this year's teacher and the child.

Another option for teachers in schools where looping is not currently practiced involves the facilitation of what I call relationship transfer. *Relationship transfer* is a structured attempt to transfer the positive relationship between last year's teacher and the child to this year's teacher and the child. In order to facilitate such transfer, the teacher who has a positive, previously established relationship with the child should meet several times with the child and the child's new teacher and discuss appropriate behavior in the new class. I usually recommend that these three people meet twice a week for the first two or three weeks of school and continue such meetings as desirable thereafter. The tone should be relaxed and issue oriented, focusing on the child's strengths, as opposed to punitive. This tone may be most easily facilitated by having last year's teacher merely "drop in" just before a transition to a new class activity or a break period. Any behavioral problems that may have occurred in the new class should be discussed at those meetings, and certainly the input of the student should be sought concerning what he or she perceives about the new class and the new teacher. Perhaps certain behavioral signals (a signal for "get back to work and ignore that student's last comment") could be developed. Only the new teacher and student would be aware of the signal, which will make the student feel special and valued in the new class.

In many cases, the very fact that the former teacher, the new teacher, and the student briefly meet can allow for some "transfer" of the positive

> For children with behavior problems, trust is a critical factor in any relationship.

relationship from one teacher to the next. This will benefit the child and the new teacher in quickly establishing their own positive relationship. For children with behavior problems, trust is a critical factor in any relationship. If the student sees that the teacher from last year has faith and trust in the child's teacher for this year, that can foster the development of a positive relationship between the child and the new teacher.

## Classroom Climate

### What Is Classroom Climate?

> *Classroom climate* deals with the emotional impact of a particular learning environment on individuals in that environment.

Classroom climate is a construct that has only recently been widely discussed in the educational literature (Freiberg, 1998; Hansen & Childs, 1998; Sterling, 1998). Generally, *classroom climate* deals with the emotional impact of a particular learning environment on the individuals in that environment. Are students and teachers happy to be in the classroom? Does everyone seem to enjoy themselves? Are academics and social learning being stressed in a positive, enjoyable way? Does everyone feel valued in the class? Do all students feel that they can contribute meaningfully to the class? These and other similar questions provide guidance into what classroom climate is.

However, the overall construct of "climate" may be discussed in terms more broad than the individual classroom. Some use the term *school climate* when referring to the relationships among students and all their teachers and/or various relationships among teachers or among teachers and administrators. The general construct continues to involve how various participants in the environment "feel" and "sense" the environment, and what they perceive their "worth" to be to others in the environment.

> The climate within the classroom and/or school will, in large part, determine the types of positive relationships that may be fostered in that environment.

From the relational discipline perspective, classroom climate is obviously critical. Specifically, the climate within the classroom and/or school will, in large part, determine the types of positive relationships that may be fostered in that environment. Classrooms that students perceive to be predominately punitive in nature will not facilitate the development of positive, respectful relationships. Students will not enjoy their learning as much—if at all—and teachers will be much more likely to burn out in a punitive environment than in a classroom where everyone feels valued and where the various attention needs of all the students and the teacher are met.

> The teacher must be concerned with how students and other teachers perceive their own value in the context of the classroom.

For this reason, the teacher who wishes to apply relational discipline practices must be concerned with how students and other teachers perceive their own value in the context of the classroom. It is important to access various informal assessments that allow the concerned educator to gauge the classroom climate in any setting from the various perspectives of those within that setting. It is not critical that every teacher practicing relational discipline use these informal measures each grading period or even each year. However, the relational discipline teacher should utilize these measures when he or she believes that consideration of the climate may enhance the relationships in that environment.

### Students' Perceptions of School Climate

Freiberg (1998) offered a variety of ideas for teachers to use for informally checking on the climate in their classroom. As one option, he suggested surveying students about their concerns. The brief informal measure, presented in Figure 6.1, offers the teacher the option of checking on how students experience the relationships in the classroom and school.

> For students who are worried about specific indicators, such as "Other students liking me," the importance of the issue will be apparent, and the teacher should plan activities to assist/alleviate those concerns.

As suggested by the relational discipline perspective, the indicators in Figure 6.1 specifically address the various relationships students may have

**FIGURE 6.1** *Assessing Student Relationships*

*Directions:* On this sheet, circle the number that represents the extent to which you agree with each of the following statements.

| | Not Worried about This 1 | Hardly Worried about This 2 | Worried about This 3 | Very Worried about This 4 | | | |
|---|---|---|---|---|---|---|---|
| Other students liking me | | | | | 1 | 2 | 3 | 4 |
| Being different | | | | | 1 | 2 | 3 | 4 |
| Having a teacher angry at me | | | | | 1 | 2 | 3 | 4 |
| Changing classes and meeting new people | | | | | 1 | 2 | 3 | 4 |
| Giving a presentation in front of others | | | | | 1 | 2 | 3 | 4 |
| Being picked on | | | | | 1 | 2 | 3 | 4 |
| Who to sit by in the cafeteria | | | | | 1 | 2 | 3 | 4 |
| Being made fun of | | | | | 1 | 2 | 3 | 4 |
| Being sent to the principal | | | | | 1 | 2 | 3 | 4 |
| Dating | | | | | 1 | 2 | 3 | 4 |
| Unkind people | | | | | 1 | 2 | 3 | 4 |
| Walking past others in the hallways | | | | | 1 | 2 | 3 | 4 |
| Making friends | | | | | 1 | 2 | 3 | 4 |
| Not having an adult who listens | | | | | 1 | 2 | 3 | 4 |
| Not knowing what is expected by the teacher | | | | | 1 | 2 | 3 | 4 |
| New teachers | | | | | 1 | 2 | 3 | 4 |
| Club activities with other students | | | | | 1 | 2 | 3 | 4 |
| Opportunities for after-school activity | | | | | 1 | 2 | 3 | 4 |

in the classroom and at school. As one recommendation, teachers might want to use this form with all of their students around the beginning of the year. For most students, the worries will not be readily apparent, and therefore most of the indicators will be marked 1 or 2. However, for students who are worried about specific indicators, such as "Other students liking me," the importance of the issue will be apparent, and the teacher should plan activities to assist/alleviate those concerns. For example, the teacher should immediately begin to formulate specific cooperative learning opportunities (e.g., cooperative group work on a major project) that will assist the student in building positive relationships with his or her peers. As another option, the teacher could subtly "preselect" a potential friend with similar social characteristics as the target student (e.g., perhaps another shy person for a particularly timid student, or another "rowdy" person for an active or boisterous student). The teacher may then arrange a special opportunity for the pair to work together.

Alternatively, maybe the student merely needs an opportunity to "Shine My Light" for the class. The teacher might only need to create an opportunity in which the concerned student has a specific opportunity to "show off" a unique skill or ability. Regardless of how the teacher chooses to respond to an individual student's need, the teacher must be attuned to such needs on the part of all the students and respond in a fashion that fosters successful relationships among students.

## Teachers' and Parents' Perceptions

> Three marks of high-quality instruction: (1) an orderly classroom environment in which learning is taking place, (2) a variety of instructional contexts, and (3) the overall sense that the students are generally happy.

Generally, teachers and parents perceive a given classroom in a similar fashion. Of course, any experienced educator can remember numerous exceptions to this statement, but in spite of that fact, I believe that parents' and teachers' perceptions of school classrooms tend to be quite similar. Adults who are looking at a school classroom typically look for three things as marks of high-quality instruction:

1. An orderly classroom environment in which learning is taking place
2. A variety of instructional contexts
3. The overall sense that the students are generally happy

With these three things in mind, it is relatively easy to identify some indicators of classroom climate that adults would typically look for as indicators of a successful learning environment. The checklist in Figure 6.2 includes a number of such indicators, and it may be used by either parents or teachers in an informal evaluation of classroom climate.

Order and structured learning is one critical component for a successful classroom, and most adults recognize this. In particular, parents realize that kids do need more structure than adults in all environments. Thus, an ordered classroom will tend to alleviate some behavior problems, foster effective learning, and build positive relationships. A number of indicators on the checklist in Figure 6.2 are intended to specify the signs of an ordered classroom (e.g., Are the kids working on their assigned tasks? and Do students usually raise their hands before answering?).

Next, adults want to see a variety of learning options, rather than a highly traditional classroom in which lecture or teacher presentation seems to be the only learning model utilized. A variety of learning options may be evident in the placement of learning centers around the class and/or interesting informative bulletin board displays. Displays of students' work also add greatly to the overall classroom environment. Several indicators are included in Figure 6.2 to give a sense of what instructional options are used in the class (e.g., Are an array of instructional activities used? Are there displays of student work in the class? and Are learning centers set up around the classroom?).

Most importantly, when adults look at a classroom, they want to see happiness in the learning environment. They want to perceive that the students are comfortable in their relationships with the teacher, with other adults in the class, and with their peers.

> Student security and happiness, are perhaps the most important factors in classroom climate.

Students, in particular, want to feel valued, safe, and secure in their learning environment. It is important to note that the emerging insights on the role of the brain and central nervous system in aggression and/or classroom misbehavior emphasize the importance of a safe, secure learning environment for the students (Sylwester, 2000). Student security and happiness, then, are perhaps the most important factors in classroom climate overall, and a number of indicators in Figure 6.2 touch on these aspects of classroom climate (e.g., Do students seem friendly toward each other? Do the kids feel like there is a bully in the class? and Do the students seek out the teacher for help with a problem?).

The use of this informal checklist may vary considerably. Parents may wish to visit a teacher's classroom prior to their child entering that class and make some determination concerning how they feel their child will do, given a particular teacher's instructional and/or disciplinary style. In that

**FIGURE 6.2   *What Do I See In The Classroom? The Relational Discipline Classroom Climate Checklist***

*Directions:*   Answer each question with a yes or no. Generally it is better to answer questions immediately without long reflection.

_____   1.   Is the teacher smiling?

_____   2.   Are the kids working on their assigned tasks?

_____   3.   Are any kids quietly whispering?

_____   4.   Do students usually raise their hands before answering?

_____   5.   Would you like to have your own child in this class?

_____   6.   Do students seem friendly toward each other?

_____   7.   Does the teacher speak respectfully to students?

_____   8.   Do the kids feel like there is a bully in the class?

_____   9.   Are various disciplinary options in evidence (e.g., rules posted, good behavior charts).

_____   10.   Are kids of different races working together?

_____   11.   Do kids often pick on one particular child?

_____   12.   Do parents often visit or help with projects?

_____   13.   Are an array of instructional activities used?

_____   14.   Do the students seem generally to get along?

_____   15.   Are most homework assignments handed in?

_____   16.   Does the teacher use a signal to get the kids' attention?

_____   17.   Are there displays of student work in the class?

_____   18.   Do the students seek out the teacher for help with a problem?

_____   19.   Are learning centers set up around the classroom?

_____   20.   Is the classroom generally pleasing to look at?

*Note to Teacher:*   This checklist is intended as an informal measure on classroom climate. It should be used only as a formative measure to enhance classroom climate, and never as an external evaluation tool. For this reason, no scoring guidelines are provided, though generally a higher number of "yes" answers indicates a more positive classroom environment. Obviously, for questions 8 and 11, a negative answer would be more desirable. For self-examination in your own classroom, after completing the form, you should carefully consider the answers for each indicator and try to identify changes that could be made to enhance the overall climate in your classroom.

case, Figure 6.2 may be used immediately prior to the end of the year, before class assignments are made. Of course, parents must realize that this informal measure is not a summation of how effective a teacher may be with all children. Rather, parents might wish to use this measure as a "discussion starter" with their child's teacher for next year, and begin a dialogue about what seems to work with their child.

In contrast, a teacher might want to evaluate classroom climate in his or her own class. In this instance, the form may be utilized at any point in the year, after students have gotten used to the routine. Further, although this informal instrument should never be used to critique a teacher's class (specifically, no scoring norms or reliability and validity data are available for it), teachers should feel free to use Figure 6.2 in a formative evaluation of their own classroom, perhaps as one component of their self-improvement goals. From the perspective of relational discipline, such formative self-assessment may be considered one mark of an effective teacher.

### School Climate Concerns

Because the issue of school climate is critical to how teachers develop relationships with their students and with each other, it is important that teachers have some type of open-ended evaluation concerning their general sense of the school climate. From the relational discipline perspective, this is somewhat less critical than the informal assessments presented previously. The checklist in Figure 6.3 is provided for that type of informal evaluation of school climate on the part of the faculty.

## Conclusion

In summary, relational discipline involves a rather dramatic paradigm shift, with effective relationships as the core concern in all disciplinary matters. Effective disciplinary practices may be fostered by joint emphasis on (1) the student's relationships, (2) the attention needs of the child, and (3) the developmental progression to self-imposed discipline standards. Judicious use of the various instruments in this chapter, coupled with regular application of the tactics discussed throughout this text, should foster a positive classroom climate based on these relational discipline principles. The result will be more effective discipline for in-your-face kids.

This book has described how behavioral strategies, in isolation, often fail because children sense that the teacher is not making an effort to establish a meaningful relationship. Although traditional behavioral practices alone do seem to work quite well for perhaps 80 to 90 percent of the kids in

---

## FIGURE 6.3     *Faculty Assessment of School Climate*

*Directions:*   On this sheet, circle the number that represents the extent to which you agree with each of the following statements.

| Not Worried about This 1 | Hardly Worried about This 2 | Worried about This 3 | Very Worried about This 4 | | | |
|---|---|---|---|---|---|---|

|  | | | | |
|---|---|---|---|---|
| I enjoy the workload here; it is fair. | 1 | 2 | 3 | 4 |
| Drugs on campus worry me. | 1 | 2 | 3 | 4 |
| Instructional supervision is very effective. | 1 | 2 | 3 | 4 |
| School violence seems to be increasing. | 1 | 2 | 3 | 4 |
| Discipline problems are sometimes not followed up in the front office. | 1 | 2 | 3 | 4 |
| Class size seems quite excessive. | 1 | 2 | 3 | 4 |
| Paperwork takes too much time. | 1 | 2 | 3 | 4 |
| I get the support I need for discipline. | 1 | 2 | 3 | 4 |
| Playground, hallway, or lunchroom duties are too heavy. | 1 | 2 | 3 | 4 |
| Professional development is rarely offered. | 1 | 2 | 3 | 4 |
| I get almost all of the instructional materials and support that I need. | 1 | 2 | 3 | 4 |
| Class periods/scheduling is a problem. | 1 | 2 | 3 | 4 |
| I feel that I don't know what is expected. | 1 | 2 | 3 | 4 |
| Security in the building is adequate. | 1 | 2 | 3 | 4 |
| Each year we have new rules and routines. | 1 | 2 | 3 | 4 |

What should be modified about how this school operates? _____
_____
_____

What single change would improve school climate? _____
_____
_____

Are there things I could suggest to the principal and/or other teachers that would alleviate my concerns about the working environment? _____
_____
_____

How can I take responsibility for enhancing my relationship with my coworkers? _____
_____
_____

schools, the in-your-face kids described throughout these chapters will require much more. The tactics in this text, coupled with an effort to build a positive relationship between the teacher and the student, provide the only avenue that may result in improved and, more importantly, internalized behavioral standards.

Although these elements are critical, the most important single factor in creating a relational discipline classroom is the *frequent reflective consideration by the teacher* relative to discipline for every student in the class. In particular, in-your-face kids will present an array of discipline problems on a constant basis, and proactive, advanced consideration of how one may respond to these situations can make the difference between success and failure with any child. With such constant self-examination and reflection, an effective relational discipline classroom will emerge, and the climate will be drastically improved in many situations. Simply put, valuing students—even the most difficult in-your-face students—is the hallmark of the relational discipline teacher.

## *References*

Epstein, M. H. (1998). Assessing the emotional and behavioral strengths of children. *Reclaiming Children and Youth, 6* (4), 250—252.

Epstein, M. H. (1999). Development and validation of a scale to assess the emotional and behavioral strengths of children and adolescents. *Remedial and Special Education, 20,* 258—262.

Epstein, M. H. (2000, October 21). *Assessing the emotional and behavioral strengths of children and adolescents.* Paper presented at the annual meeting of the Council for Learning Disabilities, Austin, TX. (October 21).

Freiberg, H. J. (1998). Measuring school climate: Let me count the ways. *Educational Leadership, 56* (1), 22–26.

Hansen, J. M., & Childs, J. (1998). Creating a school where people like to be. *Educational Leadership, 56* (1), 14–17.

Rudolph, S. M., & Epstein, M. H. (2000). Empowering children and families through strength based assessment. *Reclaiming Children and Youth, 8,* 207–209.

Sterling, M. (1998). Building a community week by week. *Educational Leadership, 56* (1), 65–68.

Sylwester, R. (2000). *A biological brain in a cultural classroom.* Thousand Oaks, CA: Corwin Press.

# Index